Narrative
Apologetics

SHARING THE RELEVANCE, JOY, AND
WONDER OF THE CHRISTIAN FAITH

ALISTER E. McGRATH

BakerBooks
a division of Baker Publishing Group
Grand Rapids, Michigan

Published by Baker Books
a division of Baker Publishing Group
PO Box 6287, Grand Rapids, MI 49516-6287
www.bakerbooks.com

Printed in the United States of America

Library of Congress Cataloging-in-Publication Data
Names: McGrath, Alister E., 1953– author.
Title: Narrative apologetics : sharing the relevance, joy, and wonder of the Christian faith / Alister E. McGrath.
Description: Grand Rapids, MI : Baker Books, [2019] | Includes bibliographical references.
Identifiers: LCCN 2018047565 | ISBN 9780801075773 (pbk.)
Subjects: LCSH: Apologetics—Study and teaching. | Narration (Rhetoric) | Storytelling—Religious aspects—Christianity.
Classification: LCC BT1107 .M43 2019 | DDC 239—dc23
LC record available at https://lccn.loc.gov/2018047565

19   20   21   22   23   24   25   7   6   5   4   3   2   1

Contents

1.

Introducing
Narrative Apologetics

There have been great societies that did not use the wheel, but there have been no societies that did not tell stories.

Ursula K. Le Guin[1]

This short book aims to introduce and commend narrative apologetics—that is to say, an approach to affirming, defending, and explaining the Christian faith by telling stories. It sets out to explore how these stories can open up important ways of communicating and commending the gospel, enabling it to be understood, connecting it with the realities of human experience, and challenging other stories that are told about the world and ourselves. The story of Jesus Christ, memorably and accessibly recounted in the Gospels, is capable of grasping our attention and stimulating our thinking—and rethinking—about ourselves and our world.[2]

Put simply, this book is an invitation to rediscover something that ought never to have been forgotten—the power of narratives to capture the imagination, and thus to render the mind receptive to the truths that they enfold and express. If C. S. Lewis and J. R. R. Tolkien are right in their belief that God has shaped the human mind and imagination to be receptive to stories, and that these stories are echoes or fragments of the Christian "grand story," a significant theological case can be made for affirming and deploying such an approach to apologetics.

A narrative approach to Christian apologetics does not displace other approaches, such as those based on reasoned argumentation, so elegantly displayed in the writings of William Lane Craig and Richard Swinburne. Narrative apologetics is best seen as supplementing other approaches, reflecting the rich and deeply satisfying nature of the Christian gospel itself. It is one apologetic resource among others. Yet it is an approach that some will find particularly winsome and welcome, including those who find more clinically rational approaches to apologetics to lack imaginative depth and emotional intelligence. Marilynne Robinson is surely right in noting that purely rational attempts to defend belief can instead "unsettle it," in that there is always an "inadequacy in argument about ultimate things."[3]

Rational argument is to be welcomed in apologetics. Yet its limits must be recognized. C. S. Lewis often notes that it is impossible to convert stories to concepts without diminishment and distortion. The ideas and concepts that emerge from reflection on the narrative of faith often seem inadequate, failing to render its depth and complexity. A mystery, in the proper sense of the term, refers not to something that is irrational but to something that cannot be fully comprehended by reason, exceeding its capacity to discern and describe. The sheer vastness of God causes the images and words that humans craft to falter, if not break down completely, as they try to depict God fully and faithfully.

In writing this book, I have tried—not always successfully, I fear—to steer a middle course between a work that is practically useful to preachers and apologists and one that is rigorously informed by the best scholarship. I set out to show that this approach is both *intellectually defensible* and *practically useful*. It is my hope that this work will help its readers assess narrative approaches to apologetics and craft their own distinct styles of approach, adapted to their own situations. There is much more that needs to be said. Yet hopefully even this brief discussion will be enough to encourage its readers to explore its core ideas in greater depth and try them out.

Why Stories Matter

We seem to be meant to tell stories.[4] Human beings have a built-in narrative instinct, as if we have been designed to use stories to remember our past, make sense of our present, and shape our future. Humans have been telling stories for thousands of years, committing them to memory and sharing them orally long before the invention of writing. Empirical studies have helped us to appreciate that we human beings are creatures who try to understand who we are, what our world is all about, and how we ought to live by locating and positioning ourselves within a framework of narratives.

To be human is to ask questions about who we are, why we are here, and what life is all about. And most often, we answer those questions using stories. And sometimes we go further, telling grand stories—stories of (just about) everything, which weave together all the other individual stories that we tell. Christianity has a deep narrative structure, articulating a grand story that connects together God, Jesus Christ, and believers.

> Storytelling is fundamental for faith because it is only through this act of telling that our story can be connected with that of God and Jesus; because this story must be told; and so that it can be told as

an unfinished story into which the faithful write their own stories and, in doing so, move the story forward. Thus at its basic level, the Christian faith has a deep narrative structure.[5]

The term "metanarrative" is widely used to refer to a grand story that encompasses, positions, and explains "little stories," providing an imaginative or conceptual framework that weaves these into a coherent whole.[6] Postmodern thinkers may have misgivings about the ambition of these metanarratives; they have, however, no difficulties in recognizing the importance of narratives themselves, realizing that it is impossible to give an account of our individual and communal lives without using stories. As cultural anthropologists remind us, there is overwhelming evidence that we use narratives to provide a means of organizing, recalling, and interpreting our experience, thus allowing the wisdom of the past to be passed on to the future.[7]

Postmodernism unquestionably has a point when it protests against the *imposition* of a master narrative on the complexities of experience, which is then used to control our understandings of the world.[8] It is, however, difficult to see a legitimate objection to the *discernment* of a metanarrative as a means of colligating and coordinating multiple stories into a coherent whole. To be told what to think is one thing; to discover and embrace a way of thinking as a willing and joyful act of personal commitment is something very different.

The Christian metanarrative offers an imaginatively compelling and intellectually rich vision of a new way of existence, made possible in and through Jesus Christ. This narrative is proclaimed and enacted by the church, understood as an "interpretive community"[9] of faith that is called into being by this God-given and God-grounded vision of reality. The Christian church can be seen as the community that crystallizes around what Rowan Williams styles "the one focal interpretive story of Jesus."[10]

10

Outsiders might see this as a *particular* narrative, characterized by its own specific rationality and limited in its implications; yet those who embrace this narrative—or who find themselves embraced and enfolded by it—realize that, although it is indeed grounded in *particularities* (such as the history of Jesus Christ), it nevertheless has *universal* significance, enabling the church to see and act in the world in a way that differs strikingly from what Charles Taylor describes as the prevailing "social imaginaries."[11] By this, Taylor means the ways in which people imagine their social existence, including the deeper normative notions and images that underlie their expectations about themselves and their social context.

It has long been recognized that narratives are ideally suited for conveying some central aspects of the Christian faith, especially the fact that we presently exist in history and are forced to think and act within it. Stories allow humans to see the contingent fragments of their finite lives within larger, more meaningful wholes. The theologian Gilbert Meilaender emphasizes this point and offers some helpful reflections on its possible implications for apologetics:

> The human creature, made for fellowship with God, can touch the Eternal but cannot (within history) rest in it. For our experience is inherently narrative, relentlessly temporal. We are given no rest. The story moves on. And hence, the creature who is made to rest in God is in this life best understood as a pilgrim whose world is depicted in terms of the Christian story. This may explain why stories are sometimes the most adequate form for conveying the feel of human existence.[12]

The Christian Bible, as has often been pointed out, consists mainly of narratives—stories of individuals who are found by God, who have been transformed by God, and who seek to tell others of God.[13] When the prophet Nathan wanted to criticize David's

11

adulterous relationship with Bathsheba, he told a story of deceit and corruption—and then located David within that narrative (2 Sam. 12:1–25).[14] Perhaps this suggests that stories have an ability to steal past our natural defenses, to disarm us in a way that in David's case was corrective, maybe even redemptive. When Christ was asked an important theological question—Who is my neighbor?—he answered it not by using conceptual theological analysis but by telling a story. The parable of the good Samaritan (Luke 10:25–37) is thus important on account of both its *substance* and its *form*. The story itself is a vehicle for disclosure, which draws its readers into that story and invites them to correlate it with their own personal stories.

In the 1960s and 1970s some sections of American evangelicalism resisted allowing the narrative character of many parts of the Bible to be acknowledged and to be treated as a distinct genre within Scripture with its own distinct capacity to tell truth and generate meaning. This is perhaps surprising, given evangelicalism's emphasis on taking the Bible with the greatest seriousness and attempting to conform its own patterns of thought to those encountered in the biblical text. With the benefit of hindsight, however, this puzzling situation can probably be attributed to the lingering influence of Enlightenment rationalism on evangelicalism during this period.[15] This rationalist legacy seems to have sometimes led to an emphasis on propositional revelation and hence encouraged a tendency to marginalize narrative as a genre, save as an illustration of a propositional truth.[16]

Happily, other evangelical voices of this period warned against the reduction of Scripture to a set of logical statements. As early as 1958, British evangelical theologian J. I. Packer insisted on respecting the different literary genres within the Bible, rather than reducing them all to a single level: "We must allow Scripture to tell us its own literary character, and be willing to receive it as what it claims to be."[17] This growing respect for the integrity of distinct biblical genres has done much to clear the way for rediscovering the potential and theological legitimacy of narrative apologetics. The Bible tells many stories; their point of convergence, however, is the single story of God, which holds them together as a coherent whole.[18]

So is one story enough to engage all of life's questions and issues? It is becoming increasingly clear that many, if not most, people use *multiple narratives* to make sense of the world around them and within them. Anthropologists have noted that no single narrative seems adequate to organize and correlate on its own the complexities of human existence and experience. Our own personal stories are a unique and complex bricolage of the shared stories of the groups or communities to which we belong,[19] even if we regard one of those narratives as being of supreme significance in dealing with the things that really matter.

The sociologist Christian Smith identifies a number of narratives that provide frameworks of meaning for people in the twenty-first century.[20] Examples of relevance include what Smith terms the "Christian metanarrative," the "Scientific Enlightenment narrative," and the "Chance and Purposelessness narrative." Smith notes that those who affirm the primacy of one master narrative still find themselves drawing on others, whether explicitly or implicitly, to provide detail, texture, and color for their rendering of reality. Many today regard any totalizing narrative with suspicion, preferring to see such narratives as local and particular. In one sense, Smith's conclusion is ultimately functional: we need a series of stories to illuminate, inform, and engage the different aspects of our experience. Yet Smith's empirical observation about multiple narratives leaves open the question of how we rank them. Which story do we allow to serve as our main narrative, and which do we treat as ancillary?

In my own case, I give priority to the Christian grand narrative, while recognizing how certain other narratives are important to some of the disciplines I engage with, such as the natural sciences. My own project of allowing theological and scientific narratives to enrich each other through critical and constructive dialogue is predicated on my personal privileging of the Christian narrative, while welcoming others into the conversation.[21] The Christian metanarrative provides a robust and reliable framework of meaning, which can be enriched or given enhanced granularity through interacting with other stories.

It is not difficult to see how an appeal to biblical narratives can inform Christian ethics. Stanley Hauerwas, for example, has affirmed the fundamentally theological character of Christian ethics, while noting its narrative orientation.[22] Christians ought to "conform" the stories of their lives to the narrative of the Christian tradition.[23] The Christian way of seeing (and hence evaluating) the world is grounded in the Christian narrative, which is affirmed and reflected in the life and witness of the church: "The primary task of Christian ethics involves an attempt to help us see. For we can only act within the world we can see, and we can only see the world rightly by being trained to see. We do not come to see just by looking, but by disciplined skills developed through initiation into a narrative."[24]

The possibilities for narrative theology are also obvious, even if some points of debate remain to be settled. For example, is a narrative theology something that uses the medium of stories, or one that develops concepts based on those stories? For Michael Goldberg, there is no expectation that "the systematic theological task must itself be done in story form," as if discursive reasoning is no longer appropriate for that task. While "an adequate theology must *attend* to narrative," this does not require that the ensuing theology itself must be framed in narrative form.[25] Goldberg argues that the major requirement expected of a narrative theology is that such systematic theological statements, whatever form they may take, must remain "in intimate contact with the narratives which gave rise to those convictions, within which they gain their sense and meaning, and *from which they have been abstracted.*"[26]

Yet there has been a puzzling reluctance to extend such a narrative approach to the increasingly important theological and pedagogical domain of apologetics. This book thus aims to both commend and defend a narrative apologetics, dealing with both the general question of the wise use of narratives in Christian apologetics and more specific reflection on the way in which the Christian narrative generates and informs specific approaches to apologetics.

It is important to appreciate from the outset that narrative apologetics does not merely remain in intimate contact with its foundational biblical narratives and allow these to generate insights of relevance to its task; it recognizes that the apologetic task itself demands the use of a narrative medium. The Christian metanarrative, as C. S. Lewis and J. R. R. Tolkien both rightly discerned, authorizes the use of narratives to communicate, express, and commend the core themes of the Christian faith. As we shall see, narrative is thus not a medium that can be discarded once its theological or apologetic insights have been identified and articulated. We cannot "demythologize" Christianity, in that an irreducible narrative serves as both its heart and its backbone. Narrative acts as both the medium and the message in Christian apologetics.

Why Facts Are Not Enough

One of the difficulties facing an apologist is that demonstrating the reasonableness or truth of Christianity does not always lead people to embrace it. Something may be true yet possess little, if any, relevance for human existence. The three statements that follow are all true and can be *proved* to be true. Yet while they might be interesting, none of them probably makes the slightest difference to anyone.

1. The annual rainfall in the English city of Durham in 1870 was 604.8 mm.[27]
2. The atomic weight of the only stable isotope of gold is 197.[28]
3. C. S. Lewis nominated J. R. R. Tolkien for the 1961 Nobel Prize in Literature (but he didn't win it).[29]

Truth is no guarantor of relevance. Veracity is one thing—indeed, a *good* thing. Existential traction, however, is something very different.

This point is of major significance, in that it raises an important question about the value of what is sometimes called "evidential" apologetics—that is, an enterprise that seeks to use historical evidence or rational argument to establish the truth of Christianity. This might simply prompt the question, "Well maybe that's true— but so what?" It is indeed important to show that there are good historical and rational grounds for Christian belief. Yet this is, in itself, quite inadequate to demonstrate that Christianity is capable of changing people's lives, giving them meaning and hope so that they can cope with a deeply puzzling and disturbing world. It presents Christianity as something external that is to be confirmed, not as something internal that is to be experienced.

The problem is that evidential apologetics fails to engage or display the existential traction of the Christian faith. To its critics, it seems obsessed with historical detail yet curiously inattentive to "big picture" questions—such as the meaning of life. There is a danger that apologetics becomes fixated on questions about the historical reliability of the Bible and in doing so fails to set out its powerful vision of truth, beauty, and goodness. As I shall demonstrate throughout this work, stories enable us to make meaningful connections between the gospel and lived human experience. We are able to show that the gospel is not merely true but has the capacity to transform lives, truthfully and meaningfully.

A point of major apologetic importance here concerns the cultural shift from modernity to postmodernity.[30] While this transition is rather more complex than this simple binary suggests—for example, it fails to take account of the importance of the recent emergence of "multiple modernities"[31]—it nevertheless highlights an important point. Back in the eighteenth century, it was important to show that Christianity was *true*; in the twenty-first century, it has become important to show that it *works*.[32] Telling the story of how people came to faith is an *affirmation* that Christianity works and an *elaboration* of the ways in which it works, which will vary from one individual to another.

Each story of this kind represents a narration of transformation, in terms of both the motivations underlying it and the process of change that ensued. It is about the forging of connections between an individual's life and the Christian metanarrative, reflecting the distinct characteristics and circumstances of that individual yet suggesting how others could make similar connections in their own ways and in their own lives. Stories have always been integral to Christian apologetics; they were unfortunately marginalized by the rise of rationalism. As the rationalist tide continues to recede, we can now recover narrative approaches to apologetics and rediscover their potential.

That elusive word "apologetics," however, needs further exploration. Before we consider in more detail the role of stories in defending, commending, and communicating the Christian faith, we need to think more about the nature of apologetics itself and its role within the Christian life.

Why Apologetics Matters

Apologetics is a principled attempt to communicate the vitality of the Christian gospel faithfully and effectively to our culture.

Apologetics is not primarily about persuading people that a certain set of ideas is right, although the demonstration of the truth and trustworthiness of the Christian faith is clearly important. It is more about depicting its world of beauty, goodness, and truth faithfully and vividly, so that people will be drawn by the richness and depth of its vision of things. It is helpful to think of there being three main elements to this task,[33] which has become of increasing importance as Western culture has lost contact with a foundational Christian narrative and failed to understand its distinctive vocabulary or grasp its distinctive rationality.

1. *Cultural empathy.* Here, the apologist recognizes the sensitivities and difficulties that the Christian faith encounters in any specific cultural context. This may take the form of responding graciously and winsomely to specific objections to Christianity or to potential misunderstandings or historic misrepresentations that may stand in the way of an appreciative reception of the gospel. The best apologist is likely to be one who knows this cultural location well and understands its sensitivities, concerns, and anxieties. She can speak its language and address its concerns in terms it can understand and respect.

2. *Evangelical depth.* Apologetics rests on the deep understanding and appreciation of the Christian gospel, which both generates the motivation to communicate the faith and informs the way in which this is done. The best apologist is likely to be someone who is deeply steeped in the Christian faith and is able to discern how its riches can be faithfully communicated within a specific cultural context. Attuned to the resonances between the gospel and the deepest human concerns and longings, he will be able to construct bridges between the world of faith and a wider culture.

18

3. *Effective translation.* Finally, the apologist has to translate the language of the Christian faith into the cultural vernacular. The Christian faith is traditionally expressed using a wide range of abstract conceptual terms that are becoming increasingly disconnected from contemporary Western culture. Central New Testament terms—such as "justification," "salvation," and "sin"—are now likely to be simply dismissed as antiquated and irrelevant, or at best misunderstood, generally by being inappropriately assimilated to the nearest cultural equivalent. These terms need to be translated or *transposed*— that is to say, reformulated in terms of narratives or images capable of connecting with a wider audience, while retaining maximum continuity with the Christian tradition.

It is important to appreciate that the Christian church has had to face these three apologetic tasks throughout its history. Every period in Christian history has witnessed the fear that the church was entering an unknown future, confronted with difficulties and challenges for which there was no precedent. Yet a close reading of Christian history suggests that the church was generally able to rise to those challenges and has passed on to us resources that we can find useful and helpful as we face our own situation. The Christian church may, I fear, have largely forgotten some of those apologetic skills that were so effectively applied in earlier periods in its history. Christian cultural dominance in parts of Europe and America in the past has unfortunately led to a growing inattentiveness to apologetics, partly because it was assumed to be irrelevant. Happily, these apologetic skills can be rediscovered and put to good use.

So why is apologetics so important? I propose two main reasons why the study and practice of apologetics matters profoundly. To begin with, it equips both individual Christians and the Christian community to deal with the questions about faith that are being raised by those around them. As the rise of the New Atheism made clear, many Christians and churches were quite unprepared to deal with the aggressive questioning of faith, occasionally amounting to contemptuous vilification, found in the works of Richard Dawkins and Christopher Hitchens.

With the benefit of hindsight, however, we can now see that the New Atheism of Dawkins and Hitchens was really a very belligerent agnosticism, incapable of proving its own core convictions and relying primarily on ridicule rather than argument to discredit alternative ways of seeing the world. Even atheists sympathetic to this movement—such as the philosopher John Gray—dismiss it as intellectually lightweight, a media phenomenon more concerned with entertaining its readers than dealing with serious questions about life.[34]

The atheist philosopher Bertrand Russell showed a refreshing honesty about the intellectual predicament of atheism. Russell was an epistemological agnostic who knew that it was impossible to prove the truth of either atheism or Christianity. For Russell, we have to learn "how to live without certainty, and yet without being paralyzed by hesitation."[35] He saw his decision to live as an atheist as a contestable lifestyle choice and was clear that other defensible choices were possible.

Yet there is still something to be learned from this encounter with the New Atheism. Perhaps we can now see that the churches ought to have been prepared for such a hostile interrogation of faith. It remains important to develop apologetic ministries within the churches, which can prepare individual believers and congregations for some challenges that might be issued to their faith and help them plan how they might respond to them. It is not too late to learn from this. Including apologetic material in sermons and adult education classes is one important way of preparing Christians to engage such challenges to faith—challenges that actually turn out to be opportunities for dialogue.

But there is a second reason for emphasizing the importance of apologetics. The finest apologetics arises naturally from a deep love of the Christian faith and a strong sense of its relevance to the world. The best forms of apologetics are steeped in Christian theology; they represent attempts to set out the rich vision of reality that lies at the heart of the Christian faith and demonstrate its transformative potential for human existence. Swiss theologian Karl Barth famously suggested that the best apologetics was a good dogmatics.[36] There is enough truth in this overstatement to require us to take it seriously. The difficulty is that many of us have a quite shallow grasp of our faith and fail to develop a deep appreciation of its richness and strengths.

Christian apologetics is a natural outcome of the "discipleship of the mind," which is such an important aspect of our continuing growth in faith. Christian discipleship engages and makes demands of all our faculties. "You shall love the Lord your God with all your heart, and with all your soul, and with all your mind, and with all your strength" (Mark 12:30). We are called to love God with all our minds, to *think* about our faith, and to respond thoughtfully and helpfully to those who ask us about the hope that lies within us (1 Pet. 3:15).[37] By becoming steeped and saturated in the rich Christian vision of reality, we find we can offer wise and winsome responses to those who want to know more.

With this point in mind, let us consider the importance of affirming the rationality of the Christian faith and the potential role of narratives in assisting with this apologetic task.

The Rationality of Faith

Christian apologetics aims to connect the realities of the gospel with every human faculty—with reason, with the emotions, and with the imagination. It is about building bridges from the gospel to our culture, from the church to society. So how can the apologist connect with people outside the community of faith? As Aristotle pointed out, rhetoric (by which he really meant an ability to communicate) makes an appeal to a number of facets of human nature, each of which shapes the form of discourse that we should use—specifically, what Aristotle termed *logos*, *ethos*, and *pathos*.[38] These three modes of appeal are regularly encountered in most forms of human argumentation, whether in the rhetoric of the courtroom[39] or in Christian apologetics. We might conveniently paraphrase these three approaches as logical argument (*logos*), personal appeal or plausibility (*ethos*), and emotional arguments (*pathos*). While Christian apologetics must never be considered a purely rhetorical device, without reference to God's grace, it is nevertheless important to give consideration to the ways in which Christianity can best connect with people.

Narrative apologetics connects with people in a way that is not fully acknowledged by Aristotle—namely, through the appeal of a story to the imagination. Neither Plato nor Aristotle seems to have fully grasped the role of narratives in expanding the capacity of the human mind to visualize reality.[40] We might use the Greek word *mythos* to refer to such a narrative, providing that we are clear that this Greek term "means something entirely different from modern definitions of 'myth.'"[41] Aristotle tended to use the term *mythos* to mean something like a "story line" or "plot," recognizing both the narrative dimensions of drama and the need for connectedness in human thought. Yet other writers of the classical period framed a distinction between *mythos* and *logos* in various ways—for example, in terms of a dialectic between falsehood and truth (especially in Plato), between the imagined and the real worlds, or between narrative and logical analysis.[42] This final approach can serve us well today.

The apologetic appeal to *logos* has a long history and continues to be important in contemporary Western debates about the rationality of religious belief. "Always be prepared to give an answer [Greek: *apologia*] to everyone who asks you to give the reason [Greek: *logos*] for the hope within you" (1 Pet. 3:15, author's translation). Oxford writer Austin Farrer highlights the importance of affirming a reasonable faith, as he reflects on the significance of C. S. Lewis as an apologist: "Though argument does not create conviction, the lack of it destroys belief. What seems to be proved may not be embraced; but what no one shows the ability to defend is quickly abandoned. Rational argument does not create belief, but it maintains a climate in which belief may flourish."[43]

The current cultural debate about the rationality of faith is driven by deep rhetorical agendas. For the writers of the New Atheism, religious belief is demonstrably irrational, in that its core beliefs are resistant to scientific verification. Yet the New Atheism applies criteria of rationality to religion that it fails to apply to itself and thus finds itself in contradiction of what most philosophers consider to be a core epistemic virtue: treating others *intellectually* as you would wish them to treat you.[44] Writers such as Richard Dawkins and Christopher Hitchens judge others by standards that they refuse to acknowledge as normative for assessing their own beliefs. As Dawkins conceded in an Oxford University debate with Rowan Williams, he could not verify his own atheism on scientific or rational grounds and was therefore an epistemological agnostic.

Yet it is unfair to single out Dawkins for specific criticism here. Other New Atheist writers are equally prone to overstatement at this point, presenting their atheism as intellectually monistic, possessed of views that are so self-evidently correct that they are exempt from any requirements of proof placed upon lesser schools of thought. Hitchens, for example, boldly and inaccurately declares that New Atheists such as himself do not hold any "beliefs," in that they only accept what can be proved to be right. "Our belief is not a belief."[45] Yet Hitchens's antitheism actually rests on a set of assumed moral values (such as "religion is evil" or "God is not good") that he is simply unable to demonstrate by rational argument. Hitchens appears merely to assume that his moral values are shared by his sympathetic readers, who are unlikely to ask awkward critical questions about their origins, foundations, or reliability. The proponents of the New Atheism seem unable or unwilling to apply the criteria by which they evaluate the beliefs of others to their own ideas.

I concede that Christianity is not totally logically compelling but make two points in response: first, that it can still claim serious consideration as offering an intellectually and existentially satisfying understanding of ourselves and our world; and second, that the New Atheism is also not totally logically compelling, in effect using aggressive rhetoric to shore up its obvious argumentative and evidential deficits. As philosophers of science such as Michael Polanyi have pointed out more than half a century ago, we simply cannot achieve certainty in meaningful beliefs. "There is no finished certainty to our knowledge, but there is no skeptical despair either. Through all our different kinds of knowledge, there is reasonable faith, personal responsibility, and continuing hope."[46]

So how do narratives come into this quest for rational knowledge and understanding? C. S. Lewis managed to combine an appeal to both *logos* and *mythos*, using an apologetic approach that could be described as an "enhanced" approach to rationality.[47] Lewis was drawn to Christianity on account of its intellectual capaciousness, its narrative structure, and its imaginative appeal. It told a story that made sense of things, without being limited to what could be understood or grasped by human reason. It allowed people to see themselves and their worlds in a new way, as if a sun had dawned on an otherwise shadowy and misty landscape. C. S. Lewis summarizes the intellectual virtues of Christianity succinctly and elegantly: "I believe in Christianity as I believe that the Sun has risen—not only because I see it, but because by it, I see everything else."[48]

One of the central themes of Lewis's apologetics is that Christianity offers a narrative that is capable of generating a "big picture" of reality, capable of allowing us to make sense of our subjective experiences and our observation of the world. Lewis does not try to prove the existence of God on a priori grounds but rather invites us to appreciate how what we observe in the world around us and experience within us fits the Christian way of seeing things. Lewis often articulates this way of "seeing things" in terms of a "myth"—that is to say, a story about reality that both invites "imaginative embrace" and communicates a conceptual framework, by which other things are to be seen. The imagination embraces the Christian narrative; reason consequently reflects on its contents.

As we shall see in chapter 3, Lewis often uses narrative strategies to communicate and assess rational arguments. However, in recent years there has been an important development in the use of narrative as a means of explanation, which we shall consider in the following section.

Narratives, Intelligibility, and Meaning

There has been increasing interest in the concept of "narrative explanation" since about 2000, especially in relation to the study of history.[49] To offer a historical explanation of an event is to tell its story, thus providing a narrative structure that allows beliefs, actions, and attitudes to be related to one another in a meaningful way. This kind of narrative makes history both intelligible and interesting by providing a framework of connection between motives, events, circumstances, and contingencies. "A story does more than recount events; it recounts events in a way that renders them intelligible, thus conveying not just information but also understanding."[50]

This idea was developed with particular insight by the American philosopher Noël Carroll, who proposed the idea of a "narrative connection" that goes beyond the mere *cataloging* of events, offering instead an *interpretation* of those events that finds ways of linking them together within a bigger picture.[51] This helps us appreciate the potential of narrative in exploring the rationality of Christianity and developing appropriate apologetic strategies. The Christian narrative has the potential both to disclose the intelligibility of our world and to establish patterns of meaning in life. Those important terms "intelligibility" and "meaning" require further discussion.

"Intelligibility" is best understood in terms of the discernment of patterns of connection between events. In the philosophy of science, this is especially linked with the concept of "epistemic explanation," understood as making phenomena understandable, predictable, or intelligible by setting them in an informing context.[52] This approach is probably best seen in "unificationist" models of scientific explanation, which hold that to understand our observations and experiences is to see how they fit into a bigger picture, allowing us to see the fundamental unity and coherence that lie behind the apparent disconnection of the phenomena themselves.[53] Narratives play a particularly significant role in articulating the coherence of our experience of the world.[54]

Now there is an important point to be made here. Yes, the Christian narrative is about explanation—but only in part. Focusing solely on the explanatory virtues of Christianity can, as Marilynne Robinson rightly points out, too easily lead to it being seen as "a crude explanatory system, an attempt to do what science actually could do, that is, account for the origins and the workings of things."[55] And if that is allowed to happen, defenders of the gospel will treat it as "battling science for the same terrain," rather than focusing on what is distinct and characteristic about the Christian faith. The explanatory capacity of the gospel is an undeserved and gracious gift; yet the real business of the gospel is about human transformation, not merely helping us to make sense of things.

"Meaning" concerns basic existential questions about our identity, purpose, and values. Science may help us with explanation; it has little to say about meaning. To speak of meaning in life is an act of rebellion against a "glib and shallow 'rationalism'" (C. S. Lewis)[56] that limits reality to the realm of empirical facts. It is to reach behind and beyond our experience of this world, to grasp and explore a realm of ideas that position human beings within a greater scheme of things, and to allow us to see ourselves and our inhabitation of this world in a new way. The general term "meaning" is often used to describe the ways in which people comprehend, make sense of, or see significance in their lives, or perceive themselves to have a purpose, mission, or overarching aim in life.[57]

Psychologists have stressed both the importance of finding meaning in life for human well-being and the role played by religious faith in providing a comprehensive and integrated framework of meaning that helps individuals transcend their own concerns or experience and connect with something greater.[58] More recently, philosophers have begun to explore how narratives help us discern or construct meaning,[59] opening up important apologetic possibilities. As we shall see, the Christian narrative allows individuals and communities to make sense of their own stories and see them as part of something greater. It is best seen as an epistemic device, which explains events by imposing an explanatory framework on what might otherwise seem to be an accumulation of disconnected events or experiences, thus laying the foundations for a "big picture" of reality. We shall consider this idea further in the next section.

Christianity as a "Big Picture"

I always wanted to align my life with what was true. Discovering what was truthful, however, proved to be more difficult than I had realized. I stopped being an atheist while I was a student at Oxford University, partly because of my growing realization of the intellectual overambition of the forms of atheism I had earlier espoused, but also as I came to realize that Christianity offered a better way of making sense of the world I observed around me and experienced within me. It provided a conceptual framework that brought my world into focus. It confronted the ambiguity of our world and human existence and offered a way of making sense of what often seemed to be a senseless world. Mine was an intellectual conversion, lacking any emotional or affective dimension.

Yet it was not so much that this or that individual aspect of Christianity seemed of especial importance to me; it was its overall vision, rather than its constituent parts, that lay at the heart of its appeal. As the philosopher W. V. O. Quine suggested some time ago in his landmark essay "Two Dogmas of Empiricism," what really matters is the ability of a theory *as a whole* to make sense of the world. Our beliefs are linked in an interconnected web that relates to sensory experience at its boundaries, not at its core. The only valid test of a belief, Quine argued, is thus whether it fits into a web of connected beliefs that accords with our experience in its totality.[60]

G. K. Chesterton made much the same point in his famous 1903 essay "The Return of the Angels," when he pointed out that it was not any individual aspect of Christianity that was persuasive but the overall big picture of reality that it offered. After a period of agnosticism, Chesterton found himself returning to Christianity because it offered an intelligible picture of the world. "Numbers of us have returned to this belief; and we have returned to it, not because of this argument or that argument, but because the theory, when it is adopted, works out everywhere. . . . We put on the theory, like a magic hat, and history becomes translucent like a house of glass."[61] Chesterton's argument is that it is the Christian vision of reality as a whole—rather than any of its individual components—that proves compelling. Individual observations of nature do not "prove" Christianity to be true; rather, Christianity validates itself by its ability to make sense of those observations. "The phenomenon does not prove religion, but religion explains the phenomenon."[62]

The point that Chesterton was making is central to Christian apologetics. Christianity offers a rationally plausible and imaginatively compelling "big picture" of reality. It is not so much a collection of isolated individual beliefs as it is a web of interconnected beliefs that gains its strength and appeal partly because of its comprehensiveness and partly because of its intellectual and imaginative resilience. Christian theology weaves together the threads of biblical truth to disclose a pattern of meaning—like a tapestry, which brings many individual threads together, thus allowing their deeper significance and interconnections to be appreciated. No single thread can show that pattern; it emerges only through the process of weaving the threads together.

This strongly visual image helps us to appreciate how the Christian faith is able to weave together the threads of Scripture and human experience and observation to provide a reliable and satisfying account of life. C. S. Lewis is one of many writers to use images of illumination—such as the sun lighting up a landscape—to help convey the capacity of the Christian faith to make sense of things.[63] Yet it is important to appreciate both that there are other ways of expressing the explanatory capaciousness of the Christian faith—including stories—and that Lewis's own rich understanding of Christianity was ultimately based on its fundamentally narrative character. Christian doctrines, for Lewis, are "translations into our *concepts* and *ideas*" of what God has already expressed in a "more adequate" language—namely, the "grand narrative" of the Christian faith itself.[64]

Christianity as a "Story of a Larger Kind"

Human beings tell stories to make sense of our individual and corporate experience—whether this "sense-making" is stated in political, religious, or more general terms—and to transmit these ideas within culture.[65] Narratives provide a natural way of organizing, recalling, and interpreting experience, allowing the wisdom of the past to be passed on to the future and helping communities gain a subjective sense of social or religious identity and historical location.[66]

But *why* do we tell stories in this way? Why are we storytelling and meaning-seeking animals?[67] If storytelling is a fundamental human instinct, what story can be told to explain our propensity to tell stories? Carl Jung famously suggested that certain "universal psychic structures" underlie human experience and behavior—an idea taken up in Joseph Campbell's influential account of the fundamental plotlines of stories, such as the "myth of the hero."[68] Campbell developed the notion of a "monomyth"—the idea that all mythic narratives are basically variations on a single great story, so that a common pattern can be discerned beneath the narrative elements of most great myths.[69] This basic idea has proved deeply influential within the film industry and has given rise to intense study of how movie plotlines conform to Campbell's basic ideas.[70]

Yet a Christian answer can also be given to the question of why we tell stories and what these might point to, which is grounded in the notion of humanity being created by God and bearing the "image of God." For J. R. R. Tolkien, our natural inclination and capacity to create stories such as the great fantasy epic *The Lord of the Rings* are the result of being created in the image of God. "Fantasy remains a human right: we make in our measure and in our derivative mode, because we are made: and not only made, but made in the image and likeness of a Maker."[71]

Tolkien is often described as developing a "theology of sub-creation," arguing that human beings create stories that are ultimately patterned on the "grand story" of God. We tell stories that are unconsciously patterned along the lines of this great story of creation and redemption, and that reflect our true identity as God's creatures and our true destiny as lying with that same God. For Tolkien, one of the great strengths of the Christian narrative is its ability to explain why human beings tell stories of meaning in the first place. The Christian gospel enfolds and proclaims "a story of a larger kind" that embraces what he found to be good, true, and beautiful in the great myths of literature, expressing it as "a far-off gleam or echo of *evangelium* in the real world."[72]

Similar ideas are encountered in the writings of C. S. Lewis. While Lewis's spiritual autobiography, *Surprised by Joy*, can be read in many ways, one of its most fundamental themes is how Lewis's discovery of the Christian narrative helped him make sense of his own identity and agency, allowing him to discern (and occasionally construct) a coherent narrative within his life.[73] Yet Lewis does not give his discovery of the importance of narrative the attention it deserves in *Surprised by Joy*, which passes over a conversation with J. R. R. Tolkien in September 1931 that is now seen as critically important in Lewis's transition from a generalized theism to a specifically Christian way of seeing things.[74] That conversation with Tolkien helped Lewis realize that myths—in the technical literary sense of the term—were "profound and suggestive of meanings" that lay beyond his grasp, so that he was unable to state in plain language "what it meant."[75]

For Lewis, a myth is a story that evokes awe, enchantment, and inspiration and conveys or embodies an imaginative expression of the deepest meanings of life. Lewis came to see that the story of Christ was a "true myth"—that is to say, a myth that functions in the same manner as other myths yet *really happened*. Christianity possessed the literary form of a myth, with the critical difference that it was *true*. The story of Christ is thus to be understood as "God's myth," whereas the great pagan narratives are "men's myths."[76]

Lewis uses the term "myth" in speaking of the Christian narrative, often suggesting that Christianity is better conceived as *mythos* rather than *logos*. Many, particularly within the American evangelical community, misunderstand Lewis at this point, believing that his use of the term "myth" implies that Christianity is fictional or false. As recent scholarship has made clear, however, a "myth" is ultimately a worldview that is presented in the form of a narrative.[77] As Eric Csapo points out, the notion of "myth" is no longer limited to significant stories sourced from "ancient" or "primal" cultures but now extends to modern narratives of identity and value, such as those of the Enlightenment.[78]

So what is the relevance of this for Christian apologetics? In his 1944 essay "Myth Became Fact," Lewis stresses that God *authorizes* the use of myth as a means of captivating the human imagination and engaging the human reason. Since "God chooses to be mythopoeic," we in our turn must be "mythopathic"—receptive to God's myth, recognizing and acknowledging its "mythical radiance," and offering it an "imaginative welcome."[79] If God chose to use the form of myth as a means of communicating both truth and meaning, why should we not do the same? Why not tell stories—above all, stories grounded in the Christian metanarrative—as a way of creating receptivity to Christianity and the great truths that it enfolds and conveys?

This short work responds to Lewis's point by exploring the role that narratives can play in Christian apologetics. It explores how we can use narratives to make sense of ourselves and our world and considers the contributions of Christian writers such as C. S. Lewis, Marilynne Robinson, Dorothy L. Sayers, and J. R. R. Tolkien who have focused on the apologetic potential of such stories. This raises some theoretical and pragmatic questions. It requires us to lay a theological foundation for such an approach to apologetics, on the one hand, and to show that it is potentially useful, on the other. We shall consider these two questions in more detail in what follows.

2.

The Theological Foundations of Narrative Apologetics

The whole point of Christianity is that it offers a story which is the story of the whole world.

N. T. Wright[1]

The Christian faith is ultimately based on a narrative, set out in the Bible, dealing with a God who chose to enter into and be disclosed within the historical process. We can speak of the *story of God* in that the character of God can be seen as *rendered* or *performed* through defining narratives that both disclose the character of God and shape the identity of God's people.[2] A narrative is not some kind of literary embellishment of the basic ideas of Christian theology; rather, it is generally the primary form of disclosure of God's identity and character, which gives rise to those ideas.

The biblical account of the exodus from Egypt can be seen as one such disclosing and defining narrative (see "The Story of the

Exodus: The Hope of Deliverance" in chap. 4); the most important, of course, is the story of Jesus Christ, which lies at the heart of Christian theology, worship, and ethics. This story is then correlated with individual human stories, as individuals try to work out how their individual story might be illuminated by this "story of God" or how they might find their own place within this greater narrative. The human quest for understanding and meaning can thus be framed in terms of this process of the "correlation of narratives."

Yet we cannot see the apologetic potential of stories simply as a piece of good luck, a fortunate accident that offers the church important possibilities for communicating beyond its boundaries. Christianity offers us a way of seeing ourselves and our world that helps us realize that we are *meant* to use stories in this way. For this reason, this chapter will explore the theological foundations of narrative apologetics, which parallels a growing interest in narratives in Christian theology and ethics within the academic community.

H. Richard Niebuhr on the Retrieval of Narrative

Many scholars trace the origins of the growing interest in narrative theology back to 1941, when H. Richard Niebuhr published *The Meaning of Revelation*, which included a pivotal chapter titled "The Story of Our Lives." In it Niebuhr argues that Christians should focus on the "irreplaceable and untranslatable" narrative of faith that straddles the borderlands of history, parable, and myth.[3] The narrative of faith is "untranslatable" in that it cannot be converted to concepts or ideas without diminishment or distortion. The original narrative captures reality in such a way that any attempt to convert this to the abstract ideas favored by rationalism leads to a dilution of its power. As C. S. Lewis pointed out around the same time, it is impossible to convert *mythos* to *logos* without imaginative loss.

Niebuhr's *Meaning of Revelation* began a productive conversation about the significance of the "irreplaceable and untranslatable" narrative that lies at the heart of Christianity. For Niebuhr, the preaching of the early church did not take the form of arguments for the existence of God but was "primarily a simple recital of the great events connected with the historical appearance of Jesus Christ and a confession of what had happened to the community of disciples."[4] The church relates its experience in the form of story as an "internal compulsion" that "arises out of its need—since it is a living church—to say what it stands for and out of its inability to do so otherwise than by telling the story of its life."[5]

Niebuhr invites his readers to reflect on the challenge faced by early Christian preachers as they tried to communicate the gospel truths about God, salvation, and revelation. In the end, Niebuhr suggests, their most effective approach was to tell their personal stories and show how these connected with something greater. Narratives relate what happened to Abraham, Isaac, and Jacob in the past, just as they express what has happened to us in the present. We exist in history and cannot escape from its limiting conditions nor avoid using the medium of history to explain what we have found—including using narrative as a tool to describe what we have encountered and experienced and its impact upon us. "What we mean is this event which happened among us and to us."[6]

Niebuhr draws a distinction between an "observed" and a "lived" history. An external spectator will see history in a disinterested and analytical manner, whereas a participant will see and experience things in an engaged and involved way. Niebuhr thus notes the importance of autobiography as a narrative of "lived" history, in which what happened is related, interpreted, and incorporated into the business of living. Niebuhr illustrates this point through a comparison of two different narratives of healing: a "scientific case history" of a man who had been blind, and who can now see, which focuses on changes in his optic nerve; and an "inner history" of someone who "had lived in darkness and now saw again trees and the sunrise, children's faces and the eyes of a friend."[7] The Christian faith is enfolded in a narrative of inner history of individuals and communities—the "story of what happened to us, the living memory of the community."[8]

For Niebuhr, this story focuses on Jesus Christ as an "intelligible event which makes all other events intelligible."[9] This is one of the most significant themes in Niebuhr's theology of revelation: an event that is both intelligible in itself and capable of making sense of other aspects of our experience.

> By revelation in our history, then, we mean that special occasion which provides us with an image by means of which all the occasions of personal and common life become intelligible. What concerns us at this point is not the fact that the revelatory moment shines by its own light, but rather that it illuminates other events and enables us to understand them.[10]

Niebuhr's line of argument is that the narrative of Jesus Christ is thus able to disclose the otherwise hidden or opaque intelligibility of other narratives—such as the history of Israel or of Greek philosophy, both of which can be interpreted as anticipations of the Christian faith.[11] The narrative of Christ makes sense of other narratives—such as our own personal narratives, or that of the church. "We need a larger pattern, a more inclusive hypothesis through which to understand each other's and our own memories. Such a pattern we have in the revelation of Jesus Christ."[12]

The story of Christ, for Niebuhr, thus offers us a "revelatory moment" that illuminates our own actions and sufferings and serves as the basis for further conceptual exploration. From this narrative, we "abstract general ideas of an impersonal character," such as original sin, the forgiveness of sins, reconciliation, and the true meaning of suffering.[13] Niebuhr's approach maintains the centrality of the focal narrative of Jesus Christ, recognizing that this gives rise to abstract, generalized theological conceptions. Yet these "concepts of great generality" cannot be entirely separated from the narrative of Christ. "Despite repeated efforts to state theological ideas abstractly it has been necessary for the church to return again and again to statements about historical actuality."[14]

While Niebuhr has little to say about the apologetic potential of his approach, there are sufficient hints in his analysis to indicate how it might be developed in this way. Niebuhr is clear that the "justification" of the Christian gospel is necessary, on account of both external attacks on faith and internal doubts about faith.[15] Nevertheless, while he resists such moves, concerned that these might amount to a self-justification of Christian communities or theologians, the seeds of a Christian apologetic can be discerned within his approach. Niebuhr's emphasis on the narrative of Christ as an "intelligible event which makes all other events intelligible"[16] suggests that the quality of the intellectual rendering of reality of-fered by that narrative can be seen as an indicator of its wider appeal and reliability—a point to which we shall return later in this work (see "Criteria of Relevance for Narrative Apologetics" in chap. 5), in exploring what we might call an "inference to the best narrative."

The Consolidation of Narrative Theology

The resurgence of theological interest in narrative since the late 1970s reflects many intertwined insights. Perhaps the most im-portant is the realization that theologians and biblical interpreters who allowed themselves to be unduly influenced by the ideology of the Enlightenment suppressed what is actually the dominant and most characteristic literary form of the Christian Bible: the narrative. The Enlightenment's suspicion of narrative, linked with its controlling assumption that history could not disclose the necessary and universal truths that were alone acceptable to reason,[17] led it to marginalize biblical narratives, seeing them as at best contingent vehicles for a rational truth that could be more reliably obtained by pure reason. Stories thus gave way to intellectual systems—a timeless set of ideas that stood in contrast to the transient and shifting world of human experience expressed in narratives.

Although a proper appreciation of the theological role of narratives eventually began to reemerge in the German-speaking world in 1973,[18] it is widely agreed that this movement has had its greatest impact in the English-speaking world. Yale theologian Hans Frei has argued that the dominant Enlightenment approaches to interpreting the Bible failed to respect or appreciate the importance of its core narrative structures.[19] The Bible, he argues, ought to be read as a realistic, unified story that invites its readers to participate in its view of reality by reenacting and retelling its stories. Frei concedes that the Bible includes genres beyond "realistic narratives," such as prophetic works and the Wisdom Literature. Psalms, Proverbs, Job, and the Pauline Letters are clearly not realistic narratives, as Frei understands this term.[20] Yet Frei's point is that even the theological conceptualizations of the New Testament—such as those of the Pauline Letters—are ultimately grounded in the story of Jesus Christ. There is thus a "narrative substructure" to some key Pauline ideas.[21]

Stanley Hauerwas has developed this point further, arguing that while it is true that the Christian Bible "contains much material that is not narrative in character," this material nevertheless "gains its intelligibility by being a product of and contribution to a community that lives through remembering."[22] And what is being remembered? The story of Jesus Christ, which is recalled through the reading of the Bible and using bread and wine in remembrance of him.

Some legitimate concerns have been raised about narrative approaches to theology and apologetics.[23] Of these, the most important is the relation of the literary genre of narrative and the idea of divine revelation. The critical issue is the theological framework within which the narrative is located and interpreted—a framework that the narrative itself may suggest or support but cannot itself independently substantiate.[24] Evangelical theologian Donald Bloesch has noted the importance of this point: "The Bible is not wholly narrational, for it also contains ongoing reflection upon the narratives of biblical history."[25] The interconnection of narrative exposition and theological interpretation within the New Testament is widely accepted,[26] allowing evangelicals to affirm the importance of narratives while still reiterating the need to establish a secure biblical theological framework for the interpretation of such narratives.

As has often been pointed out, there are significant differences between narrative theologians on various issues. One such difference is highlighted by C. S. Lewis's famous assertion that while "reason is the natural organ of truth, imagination is the organ of meaning."[27] If we accept Lewis's distinction, does the "realistic narrative" at the heart of the Christian faith concern *truth* or *meaning*? Frei seems preoccupied with the latter, whereas the philosopher Paul Ricoeur recognizes the importance of the former.[28] Yet if Lewis is right, we must reflect on the possibility that biblical narratives may engage with both human reason and imagination, with important apologetic implications.

Yet here we encounter what initially seems to be a paradox—that those theologians who have done so much to retrieve the importance of narrative for *theology* have resisted its application to *apologetics*.[29] For example, Frei and Ricoeur made landmark contributions to the renewal of narrative theology during the late 1970s and early 1980s; both, however, contested the apologetic role of narratives.[30] Frei argued that the "realistic narratives" of the Christian faith do not invite readers to assess the truth of each of their sentences (as if they were histories), nor do they invite an assessment of their logical coherence (as if they were philosophical arguments).

In part, however, this disinclination to develop the apologetic significance of narratives rests on an excessively rationalist understanding of apologetics, which leads to apologetics being seen as an inappropriate attempt to prove the existence of God on the basis of rational criteria that are not ultimately Christian but rather rest on the axioms of some philosophical system. The Christian apologist must rightly be expected to offer reasons for showing why the biblical narrative is either to be preferred to others or at least has a rightful and distinctive place among others.[31] What reasons may be given for adopting this defining and informing narrative, whether as an exclusive account of reality or as a significant informing element within a group of narratives?

The problem is familiar to any reader of Alasdair MacIntyre, who argues that the Enlightenment notion of a universal human rationality could not be defended on the basis of the historical evidence: "There is no standing ground, no place for enquiry, no way to engage in the practices of advancing, evaluating, accepting, and rejecting reasoned argument apart from that which is provided by some particular tradition or other."[32] There is no neutral, tradition-independent way in which to assess the epistemic status of a theory or belief. The intellectual adequacy of any such concept of rationality must therefore be the extent to which it is able to account for the existence of rival or alternative rationalities.

MacIntyre's point can be restated in narrative terms: if actions or beliefs are to be intelligible, they require location within a coherent tradition—and such traditions are sustained by their own distinct metanarratives.[33] We thus need to determine what "grand story" can both explain the human propensity to tell stories in the first place and identify and fulfill what underlies them in the second. Christian theologians from the second century onward have recognized the importance of showing how a Christian metanarrative is able to account for the existence of other religious traditions, as well as presenting Christianity as their fulfillment.[34]

Yet some readers might raise a concern here, pointing out that the movement loosely known as "postmodernity" advocates what Jean-François Lyotard has termed an "incredulity toward metanarratives."[35] While this is true, it does not, however, mean that all forms of metanarrative have been discredited, or even that they have been shown to be inadequately grounded. Lyotard's familiar statement is actually about the rejection of a *specific kind* of metanarrative, through which modernity has tried to give legitimacy to its absolutist discourse and attempted to ground it in an allegedly autonomous human reason.

I see nothing in Lyotard's analysis that can be seen as a legitimate criticism of a Christian recognition of the importance of narrative in the first place, or the capacity of the Christian narrative to provide a persuasive rendering of our world and history in the second.[36] Such criticism has merit when directed against a modernist interpretation of Christianity, yet the classic patristic understandings of faith were not framed in such an intellectual or cultural context. Indeed, during the early fifth century, Augustine of Hippo anticipated many postmodernist criticisms of modernity, without losing sight of Christianity's core belief that God was the ultimate referent of its narratives and signs.[37] As James K. A. Smith rightly points out, Lyotard is thus best seen as inviting us to recover "the narrative character of Christian faith, rather than understanding it as a collection of ideas."[38] Lyotard's *Postmodern Condition* can legitimately be read as a defense of narrative knowledge in the face of the increasing dominance of scientific knowledge.

Throughout this work, I shall retain the term "metanarrative," understood in the sense of a satisfyingly capacious "grand story," a "story of a larger kind" that is capable of explaining and positioning other stories, embraced because of its beauty and truth, not on account of some base desire to dominate. I have no modernist agenda whatsoever in doing so; indeed, I am critical of modernism's core assumption of a universal human rationality that all thinking persons must acknowledge.[39] The Christian faith offers its own grand narrative, which it affirms to be liberating—a truth that sets us free (John 8:32)—and unfolds a vision of how that freedom is attained and what form it takes. It is neither in intention nor in substance a *master* narrative—a "hegemonic discourse" that seeks to dominate or enslave—although it is capable of being distorted by individuals or institutions in the service of such agendas. (A metanarrative developed to serve the vested interests and privilege of some social or political group is in any case better described as an "ideology.")[40]

We need to be clear on why the term "master narrative" is so inappropriate and unhelpful as a way of conceptualizing the Christian story. First, it is not intended to master other people—to bludgeon them into submission. This is one of the most unattractive aspects of the New Atheism of Richard Dawkins and Christopher Hitchens. Dawkins's master narrative depicts religious believers as intellectually backward, socially regressive, and totally out of place in the modern world. And, second, the term "master narrative" suggests—but does not explicitly state—that God can be *mastered* by any conceptual system or narrative. A core axiom of Christian theology is that God transcends any such system or narrative.

There are other appropriate and helpful ways of thinking of Christianity as a "grand story." Reformed theologian Michael Horton, for example, uses the term "meganarrative" to designate this "grand narrative," which he rightly discerns as being of critical importance to Christian theology.

The prophets and apostles were fully conscious of the fact that they were interpreting reality within the framework of a particular narrative of creation, fall, redemption, and consummation, as told to a particular people (Israel) for the benefit of the world. The biblical faith claims that its story is the one that God is telling, which relativizes and judges the other stories about God, us, and the world.[41]

So how might this metanarrative—this story that God is telling, rather than one that we have made up—explain the origin of other stories that human beings tell about themselves and their world? Or our natural instinct to want to tell stories in the first place?

The "Image of God": A Theological Interpretation of Storytelling

As hinted at earlier (see "Christianity as a 'Story of a Larger Kind'" in chap. 1), one of the most suggestive and interesting explorations of this question is that of J. R. R. Tolkien, whose anthropological studies, particularly in the field of Nordic culture and literature, led him to conclude that "myths"—that is, narrated accounts of reality, appealing primarily to the imagination and secondarily to reason—were ubiquitous. So what theological explanation might be given for this? As we noted earlier, Tolkien located an explanation in the notion of the image of God, which he held to function as a narrative template. Since human beings were created in the image of God, they possess a capacity to create stories that in some way reflects the divine rationality that remains embedded within humanity, despite the fall.

This theology of "sub-creation"—set out especially in his 1931 poem "Mythopoeia"—led Tolkien to develop a sophisticated yet subtle theology of religion, grounded in the Christian metanarrative's capacity to accommodate pagan myths, in terms of both their literary form and their existential yearnings. By offering "a far-off gleam or echo of *evangelium* in the real world," Tolkien suggested, pagan myths could elicit wonder and longing, thus creating both an appetite and an opening for the discovery of the deeper truth that underlies all truth, however fragmentary and veiled its natural forms might take.[42]

For Tolkien, the Christian "myth" thus created intellectual and imaginative space for other stories. Tolkien's advocation of this idea proved critically important in persuading C. S. Lewis to move from a generalized theism to a specific embrace of Christianity, conceived not primarily as a set of doctrines or moral principles but rather as a controlling and informing grand narrative that generated and sustained such ideas and values.[43] Like Tolkien, Lewis came to hold that myths offered a real though unfocused gleam of divine truth falling on the human imagination. Christianity, rather than being one myth alongside many others, is thus to be seen as representing the fulfillment of all myths—the "true myth" toward which all other myths merely point. Christianity thus tells a true story about humanity that makes sense of all the stories that humanity tells about itself.

Lewis rightly saw that this distinction between "God's myth" and "human myths" offered an intellectual and imaginative framework that allowed him to see the great myths of ancient Greece or Nordic legend as echoes or anticipations of the full truth, which was made known only in and through the Christian faith. The Christian narrative brings to fulfillment and completion imperfect and partial insights about reality, scattered abroad in human culture, suggesting that similarities between Christianity and pagan religions "*ought* to be there."[44] In fact, problems would arise if such similarities did *not* exist, as this would be to imply that "God's myth" left "human myths" untouched. The great pagan myths, Lewis suggested, were

46

"dim dreams or premonitions" of the greater and fuller truth of the Christian gospel.[45]

Lewis argued that the Christian narrative thus gives rise to a clearer and fuller vision of things, which allows shadows, dreams, and rumors to be seen as premonitions and hints of a greater truth—but a truth they were unable to formulate, disclose, or embody. "It is like watching something come gradually into focus."[46] Seeing the full picture helps us make sense of what might otherwise seem hazy, fuzzy, confused, and fragmentary. It allows these fragments to be integrated within a larger vision of things, so that the fragments are joined together in a greater whole.[47] What seemed to be disconnected, random, or even meaningless is shown to fit into a bigger picture—a picture disclosed by God, not invented by human beings.

The patristic period made extensive use of the notion of *logos spermatikos*—a "seed-bearing reason," interpreted as God's implanting, through the act of creation, rational tendencies, and intuitions that were capable of leading individuals to discover God.[48] This important notion, however, is framed primarily in terms of an appeal to reason and might be considered deficient imaginatively. A new interest has recently emerged in the related notion of a *mythos spermatikos* as a way of making sense of the human use of stories to convey meaning and identity.[49] The idea of *mythos spermatikos* helps us grasp that this created capacity to intuit the divine is to be seen in terms of creating and telling stories, not simply in terms of developing arguments or rational concepts.

Dorothy L. Sayers has developed a similar approach in her *Mind of the Maker*, which expresses her own distinct view of the image of God in humanity as a kind of imaginative template, which predisposes human beings to think and imagine in certain ways.[50] The same "pattern of the creative mind" is evident in both theology and art. Sayers maintains that the pattern of human creative processes "corresponds to the actual structure of the living universe," so that the "pattern of the creative mind" is an "eternal Idea" that is rooted in the being of God.[51] Stories thus express something profound about who we are—which in turn expresses something of the God who created us in this manner. There are hints of such an approach in the later writings of C. S. Lewis, who remarked that God "is related to the universe more as an author is related to a play than as one object in the universe is related to another."[52]

These reflections give us reason to believe that stories are a God-given means of telling people about God, making sense of their worlds, and ultimately allowing them to grasp something of the relevance of God for life and thought. Even from this very brief reflection, it will be clear that a good case can be made for using narratives in Christian reflection—whether theological, ethical, or apologetic.

Understanding or Coping? The Question of Suffering

Many have noted the capacity of stories to help us come to terms with personal difficulties and cope with ambiguous experiences, such as loss and bereavement.[53] This opens up the question of how a narrative approach to apologetics might engage the "problem of suffering." Why does a good God allow suffering? Many Christian writers have written on this theme,[54] without necessarily providing the kind of decisive intellectual resolution of the issue that some might have hoped for. Yet there is a helpful distinction that needs to be made here, between trying to *understand* the intellectual riddle of suffering and learning to *cope* with suffering and perhaps even growing through it.

The central place of the narrative of the crucified Christ within the Christian narrative helps us engage with suffering as both an existential and an intellectual issue. Christian theologians have, since the earliest times, argued that the presence of suffering in the world does not constitute a challenge to its rationality nor to the notions of meaning and purpose that are embedded within the Christian narrative.[55] Augustine of Hippo (358–430), for example, set out an approach to the presence of evil within the world that affirmed the original integrity, goodness, and rationality of the world. Evil and suffering arose from a misuse of freedom, the effects of which are being remedied and transformed through redemption.[56] Augustine argued that the believer is enabled to make sense of the enigmas of suffering and evil in the world by recalling its original goodness and looking forward to its final renewal and restoration in heaven.

Other Christian writers have developed different explanations to account for the origins of evil and suffering and their persistence within the world. Such approaches are essentially concerned to resolve the mental enigmas and intellectual puzzles arising from suffering. Yet many regard such approaches as inadequate to deal with the real problem caused by suffering and evil, which is better understood as *existential* rather than *rational*. How does the story of Christ's suffering and death help us cope with life's enigmas and traumas?

Early Christian spirituality, particularly during the extended period when Christianity was marginalized and sporadically persecuted, stressed the alignment of the individual believer's personal narrative with that of Christ, especially in relation to suffering and hardship. The wall paintings of the Roman catacombs expressed this visually—for example, through depicting Christ as the good shepherd who carried his weary and fearful sheep through a dangerous world.

Approaches of this kind also dominated Christian spirituality during the Middle Ages, when there was a widespread acceptance that suffering was simply a fact of life that did not require explanation; it did, however, need to be engaged. Many writers of the age explored the question of how someone can grow in wisdom and maturity through suffering, often using images of the crucified Christ as an imaginative gateway to reflection.[57] Whereas academic theologians of the Middle Ages wrote about the cognitive tensions arising from suffering, most writers of this period focused on how believers could cope with such pain and perplexity, using them as stepping-stones to wisdom and maturity.

C. S. Lewis wrote about suffering in two of his works. In his 1940 work, *The Problem of Pain*, Lewis argues that belief in God is consistent with the existence of pain in the world. Pain, he famously argues, is God's "megaphone to rouse a deaf world."[58] Yet Lewis's reconciliation of faith and experience in this work is *rational*, not *existential*. It deals with abstract ideas, not the harsh, brutal realities of suffering and death. To its critics, Lewis's approach in *The Problem of Pain* amounts to an evasion of the reality of evil and suffering as experienced realities; instead, they are reduced to abstract ideas, which must be fitted into the jigsaw puzzle of faith.

Two decades later, Lewis published (initially under a pseudonym) a powerful book titled *A Grief Observed*. This moving work consisted of the painful and brutally honest reflections of a man whose wife has died, slowly and painfully, from cancer. One of the most moving and memorable features of this work is Lewis's description of his dawning realization that his rational, cerebral faith has taken something of a battering from the emotional crisis that has overwhelmed him. The slow death of Lewis's wife did not lead him to unbelief; it did, however, reveal the precarious nature of an intellectual faith that was disconnected from the harsh realities of life.[59]

Lewis's solution came when he reflected on the narrative of Christ's suffering and death. Lewis had been preoccupied with his desire to be able to suffer in the place of his dying wife: "If only I could bear it, or the worst of it, or any of it, instead of her."[60] The mark of the true lover was, for Lewis, a willingness to take on pain and suffering, in order that the beloved might be spared its worst. It was then that Lewis made the connection with the Christian narrative: that this is precisely what God did on the cross. Is it allowed, he "babbles," to take on suffering on behalf of someone else, so that the person is spared at least something of its pain and sense of dereliction? The answer lies in the crucified Christ. "It was allowed to One, we are told, and I find I can now believe again, that He has done vicariously whatever can be so done. He replies to our babble, 'You cannot and you dare not. I could and dared.'"[61]

Ultimately, the issue raised by the existence of evil, suffering, and pain focuses on the question of *meaning*. Is the world merely a random, meaningless accumulation of accidental events? Or may a deeper picture be discerned, one that enables the issues of human existence to be brought into sharper focus? Resilience in the face of illness, suffering, or trauma is widely agreed to be enhanced if it is seen as purposeful, intentional, or productive. The Christian narrative, which has at its core a crucified Savior, provides a framework of meaning that allows this kind of interpretation to be placed on these events, thus helping individual believers cope with their distress and anxiety. It invites us to enter a narrative that speaks of the violent, painful, and seemingly meaningless death of Christ and explores how this is shown to be meaningful in itself and capable of conferring meaning on others who suffer.

The Christian narrative frames illness and suffering in such a manner as to allow them to be seen as coherent, meaningful, and potentially positive, allowing them to foster personal growth and development. This narrative invites us to imagine ourselves as passing through a world of darkness and sorrow in the presence of a journeying God who is with us even when we pass through the "valley of the shadow of death." As pastor Timothy Keller remarks, "Suffering is unbearable if you aren't certain that God is for you and with you."[62] The New Testament frequently affirms that the

Christian hope of eternal life in the future is linked with the experience of suffering in the present and sees this link as expressed in the story of Christ's passion and crucifixion: "We share in [Christ's] sufferings in order that we may also share in his glory" (Rom. 8:17 NIV).

This brief reflection on how narratives can communicate and commend the richly textured account of reality offered by the Christian faith leads us to reflect more thoroughly and systematically on the place of narratives in Christian apologetics. In the next chapter, we shall focus on the three core tasks of apologetics we noted earlier (see "Why Apologetics Matters" in chap. 1) and consider how narratives can help us engage with these.

3.

The Practical Application
of Narrative Apologetics

Stories offer apologetic possibilities that are impossible with more abstract forms of apologetics, such as arguments for the existence of God. Perhaps most importantly, they engage audiences—such as children—who find rational dissection pointless and uninteresting yet are intrigued by stories.[1] As C. S. Lewis once remarked, a well-told story opens the imagination to new ways of seeing things, allowing the Christian story to be displayed in its "real potency," so that it can steal past the "watchful dragons" of a hardened rationalism.[2]

Earlier in this work (see "Why Apologetics Matters" in chap. 1), I suggested that there were three primary tasks for Christian apologetics. In the first place, it must engage cultural objections to religious belief. In the second, it has to show the ways in which Christianity can connect with people's lives and concerns. And in the third, it must try to present Christian beliefs in a way that contemporary culture can appreciate and understand. So how can the telling of stories help with these three apologetic tasks?

While later sections of this work will provide more-detailed engagement with these questions, it is important to deal with this general concern immediately. How, many will wonder, can a story answer a question or meet an objection? These are fair questions. While I will draw on many writers in exploring these issues, I shall pay particular attention to C. S. Lewis, who offers both a theoretical explanation of the apologetic potential of stories and suggestions for their practical application. Just as Iris Murdoch supplemented her more analytical works of philosophy with an exploration of its actual outworking in life through her novels, so Lewis enacts his ideas in narratives.

In a perceptive and sympathetic account of Lewis's use of stories, Gilbert Meilaender focuses on what he believes to be Lewis's most important achievement: showing how stories help us step inside another way of seeing our world. Meilaender suggests that this is seen at its best in *The Voyage of the "Dawn Treader"* (1952), as Lewis relates how Lucy Pevensie discovered a book that seemed to bring her close to, if not directly into contact with, something of ultimate significance that lay beyond time.

> [Lewis] tells stories which expand the imagination and give one a world within which to live for a time. Like Lucy, the reader can almost forget he is reading a story at all and can be living in the story as if it were real. Lewis offers not abstract propositions for belief but the quality, the feel, of living in the world narrated by the biblical story.[3]

As Rowan Williams has pointed out, the stories of Narnia do not aim to *teach* us about Christian doctrine and practice but rather seek to help us *experience* them alongside the characters who are caught up in this imagined yet seemingly real world.[4] Lewis's approach thus represents a decisive move away from what the philosopher Paul Moser perceptively calls "spectator evidence" for God;[5] rather than passively observing our own world, Lewis invites us to enter another world and, in so doing, come to see our own world in a new way.

Lewis's apologetic strategy is to invite his readers to step into the Christian way of seeing things, imagine how things look and feel from this perspective, and assess the quality of the Christian narrative. Does this story seem to ring true to life and experience? Does it weave things together in a more coherent and satisfying way? Would those hearing this story like to enter and inhabit such a world?

Lewis offers a theoretical account of the imaginative power and conceptual richness of narratives in several of his essays, most notably "Myth Became Fact" (1944), "Is Theology Poetry?" (1945), and "On Stories" (1947).[6] The basic principles set out in these essays are, of course, put into practice in The Chronicles of Narnia. The theme of incarnation plays a crucial, yet often understated, role in these novels, as it does in Lewis's own theological vision. For Lewis, the Christian narrative affirms that another and more real world has entered into our history in the form of one specific human being, so that the universal has become embodied and particularized, located in our world of time and space. For this reason, we need not transcend our finitude in order to find that more real world; rather, it has come to us.

Through his deft use of narrative in The Chronicles of Narnia, Lewis helps us to see things in a new way, to enter a new world of experience and reflection in which things turn out to be not quite what we thought they were. What seemed like an insurmountable difficulty when seen from one perspective turns out to be a tolerable anomaly when seen from another. The narrative enables us to see perspectives that were otherwise invisible or inaccessible to us.

With these points in mind, we shall explore how Lewis's Narnian narrative illuminates the three apologetic tasks we considered earlier. First, we consider how Lewis's approach helps us to engage what many consider to be a significant objection to faith.

Meeting Objections: God as a Projection

Perhaps one of the most commonly encountered objections to belief in God can be traced back to German philosopher Ludwig Feuerbach, who argued that the idea of God is merely a "projection" of the human imagination.[7] Religion in general, according to Feuerbach, is simply about human feelings and aspirations being projected onto an illusory transcendent plane. Human beings mistakenly objectify their own feelings, interpreting their experience of themselves in terms of an awareness of God.

Yet this objection to theistic belief has now become detached from its original basis in Feuerbach's interpretation of Hegel's philosophy and become attached instead to the psychoanalytical theories of Sigmund Freud. Freud's *Future of an Illusion* (1927) develops a strongly reductionist approach to religion, arguing that religious ideas are "illusions, fulfilments of the oldest, strongest, and most urgent wishes of mankind."[8] Belief in God is a mere wish fulfillment, an expression and outcome of human longings, representing an illusion that shields us from the harsh and unbearable realities of an incoherent world. Freud reshapes Feuerbach's argument, locating the motivation for inventing a transcendent God in a human inability to cope with life without some transcendent basis.

So how might we respond to these objections? One answer, of course, is to challenge the intellectual basis of this argument. Feuerbach, for example, makes the generic point that human beings have a tendency to construct worlds that they find intellectually congenial. If God is seen as a consolation, this indicates that such a belief might be adopted as a protection against a sense of meaninglessness or pointlessness.

Yet this argument works equally well against atheism, which is a worldview that offers human beings autonomy. Those searching for absolute freedom might wish to liberate themselves from transcendental interference. Atheism might therefore be seen as a post hoc intellectual ratification of an emotional desire. A good example of this is philosopher Thomas Nagel's atheism, which is ultimately an intellectualization of a more fundamental longing on his part for a godless world. "It isn't just that I don't believe in God, and, naturally, hope that I'm right in my belief," Nagel states. "It's that I hope there is no God! I don't want there to be a God; I don't want the universe to be like that."[9] The wish gives rise to the belief; Nagel's atheism seems to be a post hoc rationalization of his desire for a godless universe.

Or we might use a narrative approach, pointing out that if Freud's account of the psychogenesis of religious belief is correct, then his own atheism has to be seen as the outcome of his own personal history, especially his troubled relationship with his father. If, as Freud suggests, people come to associate God with their fathers, their religious beliefs will inevitably become entangled with their personal perception of their relationship with their father. "Psychoanalysis has made us familiar with the intimate connection between the father-complex and belief in God; it has shown us that a personal God is psychologically nothing other than an exalted father, and it brings us evidence every day of how young people lose their religious beliefs as soon as their father's authority breaks down."[10] Psychologist Paul Vitz thus uses a narrative approach to deconstruct Freud's atheism, showing that it was a position arrived at initially not by intellectual argument, but rather was an outcome of Freud's personal circumstances and contingencies.[11]

Lewis, however, uses a purely narrative approach to engage the general question of whether our beliefs about God are simply extrapolations from our experience of this world, including our own feelings and emotions. Lewis uses a narrative framework to allow an argument to be seen in a new light, allowing its significance to be reassessed. This approach is seen at its best in *The Silver Chair* (1953), one of the later novels in The Chronicles of Narnia. Lewis makes use of an imaginative gambit originally deployed by Plato—a dark underworld cave, illuminated only by the flickering flames of a fire. The inhabitants of that cave, who have lived there since birth, have no notion that there is a greater world beyond this realm of shadows.

Lewis reworks this idea in *The Silver Chair*, which sets out "the 'Ontological Proof' in a form suitable for children."[12] Eustace Scrubb, Jill Pole, and Puddleglum find themselves in an "Underland" ruled by the Lady of the Green Kirtle, who tries to persuade them that Narnia is simply a figment of their imaginations. Puddleglum tries to explain that beyond the dark realms of the Underland, there really is an "Overworld," which is illuminated by the sun.

The Lady of the Green Kirtle ridicules this idea. Puddleglum has simply invented his ridiculous idea of a sun, basing it on the lamps he has seen around him in the Underland: "You have put nothing into your make-believe without copying it from the real world, this world of mine, which is the only world."[13] In any case, the idea of a sun is incoherent. Puddleglum talks about the sun hanging in the sky and lighting up the Overworld. Well then, just what does the sun hang *from?*

The reader of this passage encounters a seemingly sophisticated argument, which would clearly convince any inhabitant of the Underland. Like the prisoners in Plato's cave, they knew no other world and would thus probably dismiss Puddleglum's ideas about the sun as delusional and incoherent. Yet we read this passage from our own perspective—that of knowing that there is indeed an Overworld, illuminated by the sun. The reader can switch perspectives, seeing how an argument that works well from one perspective is shown to be flawed from another.

Lewis's narrative allows his readers to flip their points of view, thus changing their informing perspectives. It offers another way of seeing things, challenging the narrative of a materialist or naturalist worldview. Unless we see things in this new way, we shall remain trapped in our underground cave, being predisposed to believe not merely that there is nothing beyond it but that there *cannot* be anything beyond it. Lewis thus creates imaginative space for his readers to place their beliefs about God and show that there are plausible alternatives to naturalism.

Explaining Significance: Narrating the Incarnation

The figure of Jesus Christ stands at the heart of the Christian faith—a person who is to be known and adored, rather than being merely the object of theological analysis and dissection. An integral element of Christian apologetics is the effective yet faithful explanation of the significance of Christ, adapted to the vocabulary and situation of specific audiences. Yet terms such as "incarnation" are now not well understood outside the Christian church. So how can their significance be communicated outside the community of faith?

One important answer is to *translate* these terms into cultural dialects. Consider, for example, the important Pauline idea of redemption, which denotes the actions through which God rescues human beings from the state of sin, decay, and death to which they have become subject.[14] Paul views the situation of humankind as spiritual slavery, from which it has been redeemed by Christ (Gal. 4:5). The analogy with slavery is not so much about moving from bondage to freedom as about moving from the domain of servitude to the elements of the universe or the law to a new domain—that of belonging to God.[15] The transference is thus not from service to absolute freedom, as a modern Western reader might assume, but rather takes the form of a radical status reversal, in which believers become subject to a new—yet infinitely preferable—owner.

Narrative apologetics, however, attempts to communicate the significance of the life, death, and resurrection of Christ through telling stories—such as those embedded within the New Testament. The Gospel narratives emphasize the transformative impact of Christ upon those whom he encountered, such as the first disciples on the shores of Lake Galilee. The earliest Christian witness seems to have taken the form of an invitation to "come and see what we have found" (e.g., John 1:45–46), rather than any attempt to conceptualize Jesus's significance and thus proclaim a set of ideas, rather than point to a person. The New Testament itself mingles narrative accounts of Christ with theoretical accounts of his significance. Although the latter are clearly grounded in the former, they take a different form, appealing to intellectual comprehension rather than personal encounter.

The central Christian idea of the incarnation emphasizes that the "God of the Christians" (to use a phase from third-century theologian Tertullian) chose to enter into the place of human habitation. "The Word became flesh and lived among us" (John 1:14). This act of divine incarnation is seen as affirming the importance of the created order, disclosing God's compassion and care for both the world and humanity, and making possible a transformation of the human situation (which the Christian tradition describes using the language of "salvation" or "atonement") that allowed those who embraced this new way of existence to live in hope.

Some will have questions about how a narrative can be said to mediate salvation—as opposed to revealing the way things really are. Many will find themselves puzzled by the question of how a narrative can have any salvific function. The point is that the Christian narrative brings us to a point at which we realize our sinfulness, on the one hand, and the fulfillment and joy of the gospel, on the other. The narrative makes us want to turn our backs on the past and embrace the gospel. The story thus leads us to want to open our lives to the transforming grace of God. To use an analogy familiar to many medieval theologians, it is like opening a shutter to allow light into a dark room. The act of opening the shutter is a human action that parallels the removal of an obstacle to grace, but the ensuing illumination of the room parallels the work of God's grace.[16] We don't cause the sun to shine or God to be gracious—but we can do something that makes us recipients of the warmth and light of the sun or the transforming grace of God.

Or, to alter the image, the Christian story might help us realize that we are ill and hence cause us to seek a cure. The story itself does not cure us, but it becomes a means by which we are cured, in that it prompts us to discover how the gospel can make us whole and hence how we can be healed by God's grace. Or, to return to the theme of the incarnation, we realize that the Son of God took on human flesh, suffered, and died in order to redeem us—so we reach out to embrace Christ and become transformed through his living presence within us.[17]

While the incarnation helps us grasp the significance of Jesus Christ for humanity, it also tells us something about the kind of God whom Christians love and worship. During my own atheist phase, I thought of God as a distant reality standing behind or outside history, detached from human existential concerns and shielded from the traumas of history. I could see no intellectual or existential case for believing in a God like that. Yet the biblical affirmation that the "Word became flesh and lived among us" (John 1:14) offers a radically different concept of God—not the abstract and remote "God of the philosophers," but a God who cares for us, not as a passive distant observer, but as an active fellow traveler and constant companion within the historical process. God is someone we can know and address in worship and prayer. Philosopher Roger Scruton has

61

expressed this point rather nicely: "The God of the philosophers disappeared behind the world, because he was described in the third person, and not addressed in the second."[18]

Yet as Christianity expanded into the Mediterranean world in the late first and early second centuries, a subtle change took place, in which vivid narratives about Jesus Christ came to be displaced by a philosophically conceptualized Christ. As a result, the identity and significance of Christ came to be framed in terms borrowed from secular Greek metaphysics, so that Christ was proclaimed as being "consubstantial" with God.[19] The biblical narratives on which such conclusions were based receded into the background, partly because the Hellenistic culture of the eastern Mediterranean region had come to see *logos* as being superior to *mythos* as a vehicle for truth.[20] Rational argument, rather than the recounting of narratives, thus became central to the apologetic task.

The Christian understanding of Jesus Christ, traditionally affirmed in the doctrine of the incarnation, is often stated in terms of the "two natures of Christ," both human and divine.[21] Dorothy L. Sayers offers a neat summary of Christ's significance, which many have found to be helpful apologetically: "The central dogma of the Incarnation is that by which relevance stands or falls. If Christ was only man, then He is entirely irrelevant to any thought about God; if He is only God, then He is entirely irrelevant to any experience of human life."[22] Yet Sayers's helpful summary of the significance of the incarnation is still framed *conceptually*. So what stories might we tell to help us grasp the significance of Christ? What narratives might we use to explore both how Christ is to be properly understood and what his significance for the human situation might be?

Happily, we do not need to invent such stories, in that the Gospels contain many such narratives that are rich in apologetic possibilities. Consider, for example, this familiar episode from Mark's account of Christ's early Galilean ministry: "When Jesus saw their faith, he said to the paralytic, 'Son, your sins are forgiven.' Now some of the scribes were sitting there, questioning in their hearts, 'Why does this fellow speak in this way? It is blasphemy! Who can forgive sins but God alone?'" (Mark 2:5–7). The narrative is set in the town of Capernaum and tells of Christ's healing of a paralytic man who was lowered through the roof of a house. Underlying the narrative is a core Jewish theological assumption that only God is able to forgive sin. Yet the paralytic is healed. The reader is left with a question: If only God can forgive, and Christ has forgiven, who must Christ be? We see here a clear trajectory from christological *function* to christological *identity*. We begin by establishing what Christ *did* and then explore what this implies for who he *is*.

The Gospel narratives of individual encounters with Christ emphasize his transformative impact—something that is best expressed by narrating what happened. In *The Lion, the Witch and the Wardrobe*, C. S. Lewis captures something of this in his description of the impact of the name Aslan on the four children when they hear it spoken for the first time.

> Edmund felt a sensation of mysterious horror. Peter felt suddenly brave and adventurous. Susan felt as if some delicious smell or some delightful strain of music had just floated by her. And Lucy got the feeling you have when you wake up in the morning and realize that it is the beginning of the holidays or the beginning of summer.[23]

Each of the children experiences thinking of Aslan in a different way, perhaps adapted to his or her individual narrative.[24] In the end, it is this experience of Aslan that leads the children—each in his or her own way—to unfold his full significance. Aslan is no "tame lion" who is easily mastered. Lewis here uses the word "tame" to imply the kind of conceptual mastery that allocates objects to predetermined categories of meaning. Lewis wants his readers to realize that Aslan is *wild*—demanding that we make categories specially created to accommodate his uniqueness, rather than trying to force him into existing ways of thinking. The old wineskins prove incapable of coping with the new wine.

Perhaps the best example of Lewis using a narrative to explain the significance of the incarnation imaginatively is to be found in a sermon that he preached in London during the Second World War. Lewis here attempted to explain the meaning of the incarnation by telling the story of a diver who is determined to rescue something precious that has fallen into the mud at the bottom of a deep lake. He plunges into the cold, dark water, going deeper and deeper until, his lungs close to bursting, he finally takes hold of the object of his quest and rises again to the surface. For Lewis, this is the story of God entering into the world, in order to take hold of us and redeem us. God "descended into his own universe, and rose again, bringing human nature up with him."[25]

It is a helpful narrative that is open to further development and exploration—for example, in highlighting the costliness and commitment of redemption. Yet its chief function is to give imaginative substance to a central Christian theme that can too easily become an intellectual abstraction. The "incarnation" is not a static and timeless idea but rather the Christian way of interpreting something that *happened*—the life, death, and resurrection of Christ—and its implications.

Yet Lewis has another card to play in this sermon: an argument for the centrality of the incarnation to the Christian faith. Lewis asks us to imagine a manuscript of some great work, such as a novel. Then someone tells us that he has found a missing chapter—a chapter that plays such a pivotal role that the whole novel turns around it. Like Anselm of Canterbury, Lewis invites us to consider a world without the idea of incarnation (*remoto Christo*)—and then to discover the difference that the addition of this new chapter makes.

In the case of Christianity, the incarnation "constantly brought out new meanings," enabling us to "notice things in the rest of the work" that had hitherto been overlooked.[26] Lewis here echoes a point made by Niebuhr, who stresses the capacity of the narrative of Jesus Christ to open up an expanded vision of reality: "Through the cross of Christ, we gain a new understanding of the present scene; we note relations previously ignored; find explanations of our actions hitherto undreamed of."[27]

Christianity tells a story about God, humanity, and the world that pivots around the life, death, and resurrection of Christ. The incarnation both gives coherence and focus to the entire Christian narrative and allows us to grasp its relevance for human life and thought. Above all, it expands our vision of reality, helping us realize that we too often satisfy ourselves with inadequate accounts of ourselves in the universe. As Marilynne Robinson puts it, rationalism ends up imprisoning us within a limited world, diminishing our hopes and expectations and failing to capture what is so important about being human: "The modern world, insofar as it is proposed to humankind as its habitation, is too small, too dull, too meager for us. After all, we are very remarkable. We alone among the creatures have learned a bit of the grammar of the universe."[28] The Christian story affirms that and unfolds how God has paid us the compliment of coming to where we are in the incarnation, taking our form, in order to free us from this restricted and restricting vision of reality. God constructs and unveils a new habitation that we are invited to enter—and enjoy.

Translation and Transposition: Visualizing Sin

Western culture has become resistant to the notion of sin. The philosophers of the French Enlightenment dismissed it as irrational superstition, fearful that people might take the idea of a flawed human nature seriously. Yet the history of the twentieth century—supposedly the most "enlightened" in human history—witnessed such violence, oppression, and destructiveness that awkward questions about a naive belief in human goodness simply cannot be overlooked. As philosopher R. G. Collingwood famously remarked, "The chief business of twentieth-century philosophy is to reckon with twentieth-century history."[29]

One of the reasons that philosopher John Gray achieved such fame with his breakout book *Straw Dogs* (2002) was its relentless demolition of the cozy certainties of Western liberalism. For Gray, "humans cannot live without illusion"—such as an intellectually indefensible blind faith in cultural progress or in the fundamental goodness of human nature.[30] Humanists may like to delude themselves that they have a rational view of the world, yet their core belief in moral progress is simply a "superstition." Advances in science and technology are driven by selfish and corrupting human agendas, often aimed at securing domination over potential enemies. "Without the railways, telegraph and poison gas, there could have been no Holocaust."[31] Many will feel that Gray has overstated his case. Yet the points he makes about the flaws in human nature can hardly be overlooked. For Gray, recognizing human limits should be seen not as a humiliating defeat but rather as a potential source of wonder and enrichment, as we are forced to be realistic about ourselves.

Some, of course, will find such a thought unbearable. Perhaps this helps us understand a second aspect of human nature—what Rowan Williams once termed a "dangerous taste for unreality,"[32] in which we close our minds and eyes to awkward truths about ourselves. The Christian idea of sin is unpopular, precisely because it articulates an unpopular truth: that human nature is deeply flawed, wounded, and broken, and that part of our problem is that we refuse to accept that there is a problem in the first place. Yet a truthful narrative has the power to release us from its destructive alternatives and offers us ways of seeing through the distortions of reality that are present in contemporary culture.[33]

How is this truth to be communicated? How can we help people to be receptive to such an uncomfortable idea, which raises deep and troubling questions about our true identity and moral capacities? Narrative apologetics offers some important possibilities. One of these is to *personify* sin, thus making it the subject of a narrative. This approach appears to be used in some of the Pauline Epistles. A good example is the personification of sin (and righteousness) in Paul's reflections in Romans 6:15–23.[34] The line of thought here is that believers were once slaves of sin, subject to its direction and authority; through Christ, they have now been liberated from the power of sin and transferred to the domain of Christ. Sin is here treated not primarily as a conceptual abstraction but as a personal force at work within humanity, whose power can be broken. This transposition from sin as *an abstract idea* to sin as *a personal force that is active within us* enables us to identify narratives of liberation that can be used effectively apologetically—such as the biblical narrative of the exodus from Egypt, to which we shall return presently (see "The Story of the Exodus: The Hope of Deliverance" in chap. 4).

Another narrative option is to tell stories that raise questions about the reliability of the dominant cultural metanarrative, which marginalizes and refuses to countenance the notion of sin—as expressed, for example, in the pervasive idea that education is the key to human self-improvement. One such story concerns the Wannsee Conference of January 1942, held at a villa in a leafy suburb of Berlin, which laid the groundwork for the "Final Solution"—the attempted extermination of the Jews at death camps like Auschwitz.[35] This conference was attended by thirteen Nazi technocrats. Their task was to agree on protocols and procedures for the elimination of Jews from Germany and the occupied territories.

Yet those who planned this event were highly educated, with doctorates or medical qualifications from leading German universities. They were part of the elite of one of the most cultured states in Western Europe. So if education humanizes people, how could such individuals have plotted mass murder on an industrial scale? George Steiner has pointed out that human beings are rather more complex than optimistic educationalists appreciate. Someone could quite easily read great poetry or play great music in the evening and then take part in mass murder on an industrial scale the next day. Steiner observes, "We know that a man can read Goethe or Rilke in the evening, that he can play Bach and Schubert, and go to his day's work at Auschwitz in the morning."[36]

Now other narratives could be brought forward to present a more positive account of human nature. Yet this does not negate the notion of some abiding flaw within us; it merely indicates the need for a more complex account of humanity that acknowledges both our desire to do good and our apparent inclination to do something that we know to be wrong, so beautifully summarized in Paul's famous reflection on his personal limitations: "I can will what is right, but I cannot do it. For I do not do the good I want, but the evil I do not want is what I do" (Rom. 7:18–19).

Yet many apologists would argue that the fundamental difficulty here is that sin is very difficult to *visualize*. It is too easily perceived as an abstract idea that lacks substance and imaginative appeal. There is an important point being made here: we need a way of grasping the reality and significance of sin by becoming imaginatively receptive to it. And one of the best ways of doing this is through narratives that engage our imaginations in order to help us reflect on their intellectual substance.

So what narrative could be told to help convey the idea of sin as a force that entraps us and from whose power we cannot escape? How can we become imaginatively receptive to such an idea? In his

Voyage of the "Dawn Treader," C. S. Lewis tells of the "undragoning" of one of his more unpleasant literary creations, Eustace Clarence Scrubb. Lewis portrays Scrubb unsympathetically as a materialistic and self-centered person whose objectives are dominated by greed and self-advancement. Scrubb sees himself in terms of a narrative in which the possession of riches leads to him becoming a master of his destiny and world, only to discover that the narrative is flawed. Instead, he realizes that he has been mastered by his desires, which he finds he cannot control.

Lewis explores the corruption of Eustace Scrubb using a literary analogy: the Norse legend of the greedy giant Fáfnir, who turned himself into a dragon to protect his accumulated treasure.[37] On finding a hoard of riches in a dragon's lair, Eustace becomes intoxicated by thoughts of his sudden acquisition of both power and wealth. In a dramatic and beautifully rendered moment, Lewis describes Eustace changing into a dragon as a result of his "greedy, dragonish thoughts."[38] Eustace has become trapped within his own imagined and self-serving story—and, as disillusionment sets in, he realizes that he cannot break free from it. Hoping that he is merely wearing a dragon costume, he discovers that he cannot tear off the dragon's skin; every attempt to do so merely reveals yet another layer of scales beneath it. It is difficult for the reader of this passage not to feel sympathy for Eustace, who finds himself in a hopeless and helpless situation.

Yet the story then takes a dramatic, unexpected turn. A lion appears and tears at the dragon flesh with his claws. Eustace does not know the lion's name; the reader, of course, knows it is Aslan. The lion's claws cut so deeply that Eustace is in real pain, which he describes as "worse than anything I've ever felt."[39] And when the dragon scales are finally removed, the lion plunges the raw and bleeding Eustace into a well from which he emerges purified and renewed, with his humanity restored. The immersion in the water of the well picks up on the New Testament's language about baptism as dying to self and rising to Christ (Rom. 6), in effect breaking free from a narrative of oppression and captivity and becoming part of a narrative of liberation.

Eustace had been trapped by forces over which he has no control. Wanting to master others, he discovers that he has himself been mastered. The dragon is a symbol, not so much of sin itself as of the power of sin to entrap, captivate, and imprison. The power of sin can be broken and mastered only by the redeemer—by Aslan, the one who heals and renews Eustace, thus restoring him to what he was intended to be. Eustace, having become trapped in a web of falsehood and self-deceit, realizes that he has become so deeply enmeshed and entangled within this story that he cannot break free from its tissue of deception. Only Aslan can break the power of this story and enable Eustace to enter another story—within which he really belongs.

Lewis's narrative serves a double function. First, it represents a narrative transposal of the Christian themes of sin and salvation, vividly and realistically depicting sin as an enslaving force that cannot be overcome by human agency. God's grace alone can break the power of sin and liberate us from its spell. But, second, it invites apologists to reflect on what stories they might tell to make those same points in an imaginatively engaging and compelling manner.

This chapter has sketched out some possibilities for narrative apologetics, indicating some ways in which narratives might be used to communicate important aspects of the Christian faith, to suggest some ways in which we can connect with the gospel, and to point to solutions to traditional apologetic questions.

Yet this raises some important questions, of which perhaps the most obvious is, What *biblical* narratives can be used apologetically? Writers such as C. S. Lewis, J. R. R. Tolkien, and Marilynne Robinson offer us a rich seam of narrative possibilities, which can easily be adopted and adapted for apologetic purposes. But what about the Bible itself, so central to Christian preaching, teaching, and personal devotion? In the chapter that follows, we shall reflect on how we might use biblical narratives in the commendation of faith.

4.

Biblical Narratives: Opening Windows of Perception

The Bible is rich in narratives, each of which can be thought of as a thread that is woven into the grander biblical metanarrative—a story about creation, fall, the calling of Israel, and the death and resurrection of Jesus Christ.[1] There is a sense in which to be a Christian is to see this grand story as defining and authoritative, challenging the rival stories of human origin, nature, and destiny offered by our world. Our own stories are given meaning and value by being interpreted by, and located within, this greater story. Apologists often emphasize the importance of grasping this grander story, seeing its comprehensiveness and coherence as apologetic virtues. In this chapter, however, we shall focus on a number of individual narratives and ask how they might have apologetic potential.

In recording his overwhelming religious experience of the night of November 23, 1654, Blaise Pascal drew a sharp distinction between the "God of Abraham, God of Isaac, God of Jacob" and the "God of the philosophers and scholars." Many have argued about the nature and legitimacy of this distinction. But one point has not been given the attention it deserves. As the Old Testament makes clear, a story can be told about the "God of Abraham, God of Isaac, God of Jacob"; the "God of the philosophers and scholars," however, has no story to tell. The Bible bears witness to the God whose actions and character can be seen in history and hence can be expressed in the form of a narrative.

Biblical narratives generally involve an interweaving of history and interpretation, mingling a narration of events with an assessment of their significance. At times, this poses some challenges to the reader. For example, is the "Succession narrative" beginning in 1 Kings to be understood as supporting Solomon's claim to be the legitimate successor of David, or as critical of Solomon's claims to be king of Israel, or as inviting its readers to face up to the moral and personal tensions within Solomon and learn to live with them?[2] Other Old Testament narratives—such as the defining stories of the exodus from Egypt and the exile in Babylon—are better understood, especially in relation to their capacity to generate an intellectual map of reality. Both of these will be considered in the present chapter.

Although this chapter will give due attention to historical and theological issues, its primary focus is apologetic. In what way does telling the four stories to be considered in this chapter open up apologetic possibilities? How do these narratives create a framework for exploring the conceptual vitality and existential traction of the Christian faith? How can they be windows of perception for those struggling to grasp what Christianity is all about? Limits of space mean that we can focus on only four case studies, but readers can easily extend this list and develop others for their own purposes. This chapter aims to open up discussion through selective illustration and allow readers to develop these ideas further.

In each of these biblical narratives, the reader is invited to step inside these stories and see the world from within them.[3] These narratives are like windows, allowing us to see ourselves and our world in a Christian way and inviting us to assess the quality and texture of their rendering of reality. How do they help us make sense of experience? How do they help us understand what has gone wrong and what can be done to put it right? How do they engender hope? Traditionally, apologetics rightly reaffirms the fundamental historicity of the great events of the biblical past—such as the exodus and exile. Yet we are also invited to assess the reliability and trustworthiness of these narratives by reflecting on the quality of their accounts of observation and experience and the manner in which these are held together.

Some may, however, raise a concern here. Surely a better apologetic strategy is to draw on stories taken from culture at large, rather than specifically Christian stories? And does not drawing on biblical narratives raise further questions about biblical authority and interpretation? Some fair points are being made here. Yet one of the core objectives of narrative apologetics is to familiarize our audiences with some core biblical stories and invite them to taste the quality of their rendering of experience. In telling these stories, we are not initially asking people to accept their authority but rather are inviting them to explore the way of seeing reality that they open up.

Such a process of reflection also leads people to reflect on the plausibility of other narratives, including those privileged by Western culture that, in effect, control public discussion of issues such as the place of faith in public life. A form of groupthink emerges, which privileges a single narrative of human existence—such as what Christian Smith has identified as the "Scientific Enlightenment narrative" (see "Why Stories Matter" in chap. 1). Ludwig Wittgenstein has pointed out how easily a single way of thinking can come to dominate social discussion, so that our imaginations become so fixated on one specific way of seeing things that it proves difficult for us to liberate ourselves from its imaginative thrall: "A *picture* held us captive."[4]

Wittgenstein rightly notes how easily our understanding of our world can be shaped by an "organizing myth"[5]—a metanarrative that has, whether we realize it or not, come to dominate our perception of our world, in effect predisposing us to regard certain interpretations of experience as natural or self-evidentially correct, while blinding us to alternative ways of understanding it. Charles Taylor makes a similar point, noting how such a metanarrative often gains the cultural ascendancy through historical contingency rather than intellectual excellence.[6] Wittgenstein thus suggests that we need to free ourselves from the grip of such pictures or narratives,[7] considering alternatives that might offer a better rendering of our world—such as those offered by the four biblical narratives we shall consider in this chapter.

With this point in mind, we turn to reflect on the first of these narratives—the exodus from Egypt.

The Story of the Exodus: The Hope of Deliverance

Our first narrative case study is the exodus from Egypt, widely seen as a pivotal moment in the emergence of the distinct ethnic group known as "the people of Israel." Parallel accounts of this event are known, originating from non-Jewish sources. For example, Hecataeus of Abdera, writing around 320 BC, refers to a "great plague" afflicting Egypt "in ancient times," leading to the expulsion of foreigners, many of whom settled in the land known as Judea.[8] While the historical details of both the exodus and the subsequent conquest of Canaan remain unclear,[9] there is agreement that the cultural memory of the exodus—affirmed and consolidated through the Passover ritual—was of critical importance in the fashioning of Israel's identity and above all in shaping its understanding of its God.

The narrative of the exodus extends, of course, to include the period of "wilderness wandering" and the entry into the promised land.

The exodus narrative functions at several levels in the Old Testament, serving as a reminder of the historical origins of Israel and an affirmation of the activity and benevolence of Israel's God. Perhaps the most striking feature is the way in which God is named with reference to this narrative. The covenant God of Israel is identified as the one who delivered Israel from captivity in Egypt. "Remember that you were a slave in the land of Egypt, and the LORD your God brought you out from there with a mighty hand and an outstretched arm" (Deut. 5:15).[10] Israel's God is the one who stands at the heart of this narrative of redemption and deliverance.

Some Jewish writers living in Egypt during the intertestamental period tended to reinterpret the exodus narrative in light of the prevailing Hellenistic culture. Philo of Alexandria, for example, understood the exodus as more than a narrative about the escape from Egypt, seeing it primarily as an allegory for the journey of the soul.[11] But what did this narrative mean to the first Christians? Most of them were not Jewish, so how did they establish a personal and meaningful connection with this Jewish narrative of the exodus from Egypt? The evidence clearly indicates that early Christian writers quickly appreciated the theological significance of this story and were able to anchor it firmly within the Christian metanarrative using typological exegesis.

"Typology" is the search for correspondence between events, persons, or things within the historical framework of revelation, so that the Old Testament is seen to anticipate the events and ideas of the New Testament.[12] Typological exegesis secured the theological connection of the old and the new covenants by proposing a correlation of "type" and "antitype"—the anticipation and fulfillment, the shadow and the reality. Second-century theologian Melito of Sardis thus developed the idea that the Passover is to be seen as a "type" of the death of Christ. The Passover once celebrated in Egypt is to be seen as prefiguring "Christ our Passover" (1 Cor. 5:7 NASB), just as the Passover lamb slain in Egypt anticipates the "Lamb slain from the foundation of the world" (Rev. 13:8 KJV). Similarly, the history of Israel in Egypt is to be seen as an anticipation of the history of Jesus Christ in Judea, while the history of Jesus in Judea is to be seen as a recapitulation of the history of Israel in Egypt. Christians could thus see the exodus as part of their own family history, linking believers and the community of faith with God's saving acts in the past.

Seeing the exodus as a "type" allowed a theological link to be developed between the past and the present, through which the realities of present experience could be connected with the biblical narrative of God's past actions and thus be *understood* and potentially *transformed*. Augustine of Hippo's christological reading of the Old Testament allowed him to transcend the historical specifics of the history of Israel,[13] opening up a grand vista of the nature and destiny of humanity within the cosmos. Similar approaches are found in leading theologians and preachers of the early church, such as John Chrysostom: "The Israelites passed through the sea; you have passed from death to life. They were delivered from the Egyptians; you have been delivered from the powers of darkness. The Israelites were freed from slavery to a pagan people; you have been freed from the much greater slavery to sin."[14]

As interpreted by Christians, the exodus narrative thus "symbolizes something basic about the universe,"[15] to borrow a phrase from the famous sermon "The Death of Evil upon the Seashore," preached by Martin Luther King Jr. in 1954. For King, as for so many early Christian writers, the exodus narrative could be read in a way that provided a lens through which the truth about the human situation was disclosed and the possibility of divine transformation of that situation was proclaimed. The apologetic potential of this biblical narrative thus lies not primarily in its historical factuality but in its capacity to provide a truthful and compelling account of human existence.

Philosopher Mary Midgley offers us an image that is helpful in appreciating the apologetic potential of biblical narratives. She argues that we need "multiple maps" of our world if we are to grasp and appreciate its complexity.[16] No single angle of approach or way of looking at things is good enough on its own to render the complexity of nature. Midgley's point is easily grasped by considering the multiple ways in which we try to make sense of human nature, the complexity of which calls out for "inter-disciplinary cross-fertilization"[17]—something that can be achieved through the coordination of multiple maps. One map might help us understand our biological function and location; another might help us understand our true nature and destiny. We need both of these maps if we are to inhabit this world meaningfully. This basic principle can also be applied to biblical narratives. One map is *historical*, in effect telling us what happened; the other is *theological and existential*, telling us what these events meant at the time and might mean for us now. This second map allows us to appreciate the significance of these events for our understanding of God and for the illumination and redemption of human nature.

Early Christian writers realized that the exodus narrative provided an imaginative template for the interpretation of human experience. They had no doubt of the deep appeal of the exodus narrative to the human imagination and of its reflection of the experienced realities of life—such as a pervasive sense of hopelessness and alienation. The narrative of the exodus in its expanded form, which includes the wilderness wanderings and the crossing of the Jordan into Canaan, provides a map of the landscape of faith, which has found a rich tradition of application in Christian spirituality.[18]

So how can this narrative be used to elicit interest in Christianity and create imaginative receptivity to its themes? The simplest answer to this question is this: we need to enter into the narrative, stepping inside it and seeing things from its perspective—and being willing to embrace the greater narrative of which this is part, allowing our own stories to become part of this grander vision of reality.

This narrative begins by describing the condition of humanity. We are in bondage, trapped in a situation that is not of our own choosing and from which we cannot break free. We are characters in a story that we did not write and so cannot control. We are the slaves of the "elemental spirits of the universe" (Col. 2:8), which we do not consider legitimate, and which do not have our own interests at heart. We long for a liberation that seems to lie beyond our grasp, through which we might become the people whom we sense we are meant to be. We are, in short, in Egypt, hoping for our own promised land. Where we are is not where we are meant to be. We belong somewhere else—somewhere that lies beyond us. So where is this land to be found? And who will deliver us?

The Christian reading of the exodus narrative thus leads into the "good news" of Christ as the new Moses, who liberates human beings from bondage and journeys with them as they prepare to cross the Jordan and enter into the new promised land. It thus affirms both the human need for redemption and the existence of a redeemer who is able to break the power of sin and also holds out the hope of heaven after our period of wandering in this world. Finally, it invites us to step into this narrative and make it our own. Apologetics could thus be seen as an invitation to "taste and see that the LORD is good" (Ps. 34:8), sampling the spiritual quality of the Christian rendering of reality and considering what this implies in terms of its intellectual trustworthiness.

The Story of the Exile: Where Do We Really Belong?

The second biblical narrative is that of the exile of the people of Jerusalem in the great city of Babylon—probably the largest city in the world at the time. In the sixth century before Christ, Jerusalem was the small capital city of the sparsely populated kingdom of Judah, which found itself caught up in the struggle between Egypt and the Babylonian Empire for control of the eastern Mediterranean. Although many aspects of this event (including the precise number of people deported to Babylon) remain unclear,[19] there is no doubt of the theological significance that was attached to the period of exile by later writers of the Old Testament.[20]

The historical narrative of the exile begins with the tensions that emerged within the ruling elite of Jerusalem following the death of Josiah, king of Judah, in 609 BC. Following the defeat of the Assyrian Empire in 605, Judah had to make a decision about which of the two major regional powers it should support—Egypt or the Babylonians. Initially, Judah chose to ally itself with the Babylonian Empire. Yet while Nebuchadnezzar defeated an Egyptian army at Carchemish in 605, he was in turn defeated by the Egyptians in 601. This prompted Judah to review its commitments. Its decision to rebel against Babylon resulted in the occupation of its territories and the besieging of Jerusalem in 597 BC. Some prominent citizens of Jerusalem were deported at that time, and the city reverted to Babylonian rule. Following a second revolt in 594, a renewed Babylonian assault on the cities of Judah, including Jerusalem, resulted in the destruction of the Jerusalem temple and many other buildings and the deportation of several thousand of the population of the city to Babylon in 587.

Meanwhile, a new empire began to emerge in the region. Under Cyrus the Great, the Achaemenid Empire (also known as the Persian Empire) began to emerge. After conquering Lydia and Media, Cyrus turned his attention to the Babylonian Empire. Babylon finally fell to Cyrus the Persian in 539 BC. Shortly afterward, Cyrus issued a general decree permitting foreigners who had been deported to Babylon to return home. Some of the Jews made the long return journey to Jerusalem; others, however, chose to remain in Babylon.

The Old Testament prophets tended to see the exile both as a punishment for Israel's disobedience and as an opportunity to rebuild and purify the Jewish religion.[21] Yet the apologetic application of this narrative involves moving beyond the question of the significance of the exile for the history of Israel and the emergence of Jewish self-identity and consider how this story illuminates the universal human situation today.

While there are several ways in which the narrative of exile can be developed apologetically, perhaps the most winsome and engaging of these is to correlate it with the deep sense of metaphysical disquiet that many people experience, often expressed in terms of a sense that we don't really belong here. This perception is well attested throughout human history and is arguably reflected in the rise of gnosticism in late classical antiquity. Although gnosticism is not really a coherent philosophical or religious system, it possesses certain characteristic traits, such as a sense of alienation or disconnectedness from the world, reflecting a deeper intuition that this is not where we really belong.[22] We find ourselves trapped in this world, as "gold in the mud," knowing that we really belong somewhere else.

Yet this sense of belonging elsewhere is by no means limited to gnosticism. Perhaps one of the finest statements of this sense of being lost in a place in which we do not really belong is that of the Christian philosopher Pascal:

> When I consider the short duration of my life, swallowed up in the eternity before and after, the little space which I fill, and even can see,

engulfed in the infinite immensity of spaces of which I am ignorant, and which know me not, I am frightened, and am astonished at being here rather than there; for there is no reason why here rather than there, why now rather than then. Who has put me here? By whose order and direction have this place and time been allotted to me?[23]

G. K. Chesterton also knew of this sense of existential unease and expressed it pithily in one of his neatest aphorisms: "We have come to the wrong star. . . . That is what makes life at once so splendid and so strange. . . . The true happiness is that we *don't* fit. We come from somewhere else. We have lost our way."[24] The same basic idea is expressed in the existentialist notion of *Geworfenheit* (literally, "thrownness"), introduced by German philosopher Martin Heidegger to refer to the frustration of being "thrown into the world" and being enmeshed within constraints not of our own choosing. This theme is often echoed in popular culture—for example, in the lyrics to one of the songs of the American rock band The Doors: "Into this world we're thrown."[25] We did not choose to be born in this world and wonder whether we can find our way to a better place.

The narrative of the exile invites us to imagine ourselves as one of the people of Jerusalem living in Babylon, treasuring the memories of a lost Jerusalem and longing to return there. "By the rivers of Babylon—there we sat down and there we wept when we remembered Zion" (Ps. 137:1). The people of Jerusalem had been thrown into Babylon, where they did not belong; their true identity lay in their lost homeland, to which they longed to return.[26] In our own case, we are invited to see Babylon not as the ancient city but as an existential place into which we find ourselves thrown, and which is not of our own choosing—a trope widely used in literature, as in F. Scott Fitzgerald's short story "Babylon Revisited" (1931), focusing on a cultural sense of dislocation and alienation.[27]

While the New Testament does not explicitly engage the "exile" theme,[28] it nevertheless develops several related narratives focusing on the theme of not really belonging in this world. The most interesting of these is the implicit appeal to the Roman concept of a *colonia* in Paul's letter to the Philippians. "Our citizenship is in heaven, and it is from there that we are expecting a Savior, the Lord Jesus Christ" (Phil. 3:20).[29] Philippi (named after the father of Alexander the Great) was annexed by the Romans in 148 BC, and in New Testament times it was populated by Roman citizens and governed according to Roman law.[30] Roman citizens residing in Philippi had the right to return home to the metropolis after their service in the colony. They might *live* in Philippi, yet they *belonged* in Rome. Philippi was not their true homeland.

A Christian reading of the exile narrative thus engages directly with this sense of alienation and dislocation, offering an interpretative framework that allows us to see ourselves in exile in this world. It is not our true homeland but rather a place into which we have been thrown. Our quest is to find our way back to where we are *meant* to be. We are "strangers and sojourners" (Lev. 25:23 KJV), people who pass through this world but do not belong there. The Christian reading of the exile narrative thus begins a process of reflection by affirming that this world is not our true homeland, resonating with this sense of existential unease.

Yet this Christian narrative moves on to affirm that we really belong in heaven. This, of course, is a leading theme in the sermons and homilies of many early Christian writers. This status of belonging is articulated in various ways. We might think, for example, of Cyprian of Carthage's famous declaration that "paradise is our homeland [Latin: *patria*]." However, the New Testament tends to focus on the status of Christians as "citizens of heaven" (e.g., Phil. 3:20–21), an image that implies the right to dwell there, grounded in the work of Christ. As the *Epistle to Diognetus* puts it, Christians "pass their days on earth, but they are citizens of heaven."[31] A famous hymn by the medieval theologian Peter Abelard captures the existential and spiritual implications of this dialectic between our place of exile and our true homeland:

> Now, in the meanwhile, with hearts raised on high,
> We for that country must yearn and must sigh;
> Seeking Jerusalem, dear native land,
> Through our long exile on Babylon's strand.[32]

Christian apologists have often pointed out that human experience is shot through with hints that this world is not our true home. This is a leading theme, for example, in the writings of C. S. Lewis,[33] who suggested that we see this world as an inn, a resting place, but not our real home. Lewis's gradual move away from atheism toward Christianity reflected his growing realization that atheism lacked real intellectual substance and seemed imaginatively impoverished. Lewis had been haunted by a deep intuition that his minimalist atheism failed to do justice to the complexities of the universe. He found himself reflecting on the possible implications of a deep and elusive sense of longing that was heightened rather than satisfied by what he found around him.

Lewis came to the conclusion that this longing pointed to something beyond the boundaries of human knowledge and experience: "If I find in myself a desire which no experience in this world can satisfy, the most probable explanation is that I was made for another world."[34] For Lewis, heaven was to be thought of as a realm beyond the limits of present human experience, yet which was signposted by our deepest intuitions and experiences. It was like hearing the sound of music faintly, coming from across the distant hills, or catching the scent of a far-off flower, wafted by a passing breeze. Lewis came to see such experiences as "arrows of Joy," a wake-up call to discover and experience this deeper vision of reality, in which our true destiny is seen to lie beyond the world we now know and inhabit.[35] This hope is expressed particularly well in some lines from *The Last Battle,* the concluding novel of The Chronicles of Narnia. On seeing the "new Narnia," Jewel the Unicorn declares: "I have come home at last! This is my real country! I belong here. This is the land I have been looking for all my life, though I never knew it till now."[36]

The classic Christian retelling of the exile narrative offers a narrated worldview—that is to say, a way of understanding ourselves that is conveyed through a story and makes its appeal primarily to the imagination and secondarily to reason. It establishes a network of connections with human experience—such as the intuition that we do not really belong here, a sense of alienation and disconnection from this world, and a sense that there is something beyond the everyday realm, which is hinted at within that realm. This narrative thus diagnoses what is wrong and offers a solution—initially through realizing what our true situation is, and subsequently by enabling us to embrace through faith the new way of living and hoping that the gospel makes possible.

The Story of Jesus Christ: Rendering the Love of God

Having considered two classic narratives from the history of Israel, we turn to the New Testament for our third example of a biblical narrative with apologetic potential. There is no doubt about which narrative provides fundamental unity and coherence for the New Testament: the story of Jesus Christ. As Emil Brunner pointed out, the Christian understanding of Christ as both revealer and savior is not set out in the Gospels in the form of doctrines but is rather presented in the form of a story (*Geschichte*).[37] For Brunner, the most fundamental insight of the Christian faith is that "Jesus Christ is the content of faith and of truth." Whereas Greek philosophy thought of truth as something that was timeless and changeless, biblical writers understand truth primarily as something that *happened*.[38]

The New Testament and the long tradition of Christian reflection on its foundational documents both affirm that God entered into the world of time and space in Jesus Christ. "The Word became flesh and lived among us, and we have seen his glory" (John 1:14). Once this truth is grasped, the importance of narrative for understanding the full significance of Jesus Christ becomes obvious. If God entered human history, when did this happen? Where did this happen? What did this look like? Who saw this happen? Answering these questions demands a story—a narration of the entry of God into our world by those who witnessed it and appreciated its significance. "We declare to you what was from the beginning, what we have heard, what we have seen with our eyes, what we have looked at and touched with our hands, concerning the word of life—this life was revealed, and we have seen it and testify to it, and declare to you the eternal life that was with the Father and was revealed to us" (1 John 1:1–2).

Stories, of course, need interpretation. What do they mean? Having told the full story of Christ, we move on to reflect on its implications for our understanding of God and ourselves. There is ample evidence of the "communal reading" of texts such as what we now know as the Gospels in early Christianity.[39] Telling (or retelling) the story is an invitation to enter and appropriate that story, thus making it our own. The best way of communicating the significance of Jesus Christ is thus not to explain the doctrine of the "two natures" of Christ set out by the Council of Chalcedon (451), but to retell parts of the story of Christ (hence engaging the imagination) and then reflect on its significance for our understanding of his significance—and so make connections with the needs, longings, and concerns of our audiences.

It is thus important to ask a historical question, so easily over-looked: Why did so many people become Christians in the first few centuries of our era?[40] What did they find in it? How did it connect with their lives? What did it offer that they failed to find elsewhere? And how might we use such insights in our own cultural context? To appreciate both the imaginative power of narrative apologetics in general and the particular importance of the foundational story of Jesus Christ, we shall briefly explore the way in which narratives render the character of the "God and Father of our Lord Jesus Christ" (Eph. 1:3; 1 Pet. 1:3) in ways that capture the human imagination more effectively than the mere enunciation of Christian ideas.

Consider the question of how we speak of the "love of God" to seekers and outsiders, based on this New Testament text: "God is love [*agapē*]. God's love was revealed among us in this way: God sent his only Son into the world so that we might live through him. In this is love, not that we loved God but that he loved us and sent his Son to be the atoning sacrifice for our sins" (1 John 4:8–10). This familiar passage makes two distinct types of statement about the love of God. The first is framed almost as a timeless ahistorical truth: "God is love." It is an important theological insight that is woven into the fabric of Christian theology. Think, for example, of the Christian interpretation of the cross of Christ, traditionally explored using "theories of the atonement." John Stott ably identifies the central role of the motif of the love of God in such theories: "It cannot be emphasized too strongly that God's love is the source, not the consequence, of the atonement. . . . God does not love us because Christ died for us; Christ died for us because God loved us."[41]

Yet there is an apologetic issue here that concerns the manner of *presentation* of this theme, not its veracity. To some, the love of God will seem to be presented and explored in a theoretical and abstract manner, which appeals primarily to the mind rather than the imagination. We are assured that "God is love," but some will be left unsure what this word "love" means and how it is shown. What seems like the affirmation of a timeless theological principle will doubtless help some to think about divine love; others, however, will simply not get what it is all about.

So we turn to the second of those theological statements: "God sent his only Son into the world so that we might live through him." It is impossible to miss the dramatic change in imagery and genre that takes place here. The focus shifts from generalized abstractions to the specifics of human history. Metaphysics is replaced by a *narrative*. We are told what God *did* in human history to demonstrate both the nature and the constancy of the divine love, thus expanding and enriching the broader earlier declaration that "God is love," allowing this to connect with our imaginations and emotions. Might John have a dual readership in mind—a Greek audience comfortable with metaphysical ideas and a Jewish readership attuned to narratives?

The statement that "God sent his only Son into the world" thus evokes the memory of the greater Gospel narrative, which speaks so powerfully of the love of God for us. It calls to mind the Gospel accounts of the passion of Christ, which highlight both the reality of that suffering and the reason for Christ's willingness to bear it: his obedience to God and his love for us. It invites us to turn over in our minds and savor elements of that narrative, seeing in our mind's eye the shocking scene of Christ's crucifixion. The Passion Narratives draw us into that appalling scene, emphasizing the costliness of our redemption.

One element of that narrative will help make the critical point about the capacity of a narrative to draw us into its world and challenge us to experience and understand what is happening and its deeper significance. As Christ was dying on the cross, he was ridiculed by those standing around him:

Those who passed by derided him, shaking their heads and saying, "Aha! You who would destroy the temple and build it in three days, save yourself, and come down from the cross!" In the same way the chief priests, along with the scribes, were also mocking him among themselves and saying, "He saved others; he cannot save himself." (Mark 15:29–31)

Yet Christ did not come down from the cross and save himself; he stayed there and saved us instead. John both recalls this narrative and brings home its theological and apologetic significance: God "loved us and sent his Son to be the atoning sacrifice for our sins."

So what is the love of God like? A narrative approach to apologetics tells us that it is disclosed in the story of Christ laying down his life so that those whom he loves might live (cf. John 15:13). The Passion Narrative has its own distinct integrity and deep appeal, which the apologist is called on to reflect and exhibit. Instead of appealing primarily to an abstract timeless truth, the apologist can retell the story of the passion of Christ, inviting the listeners to enter into that narrative and try to understand both what is going on and how it relates to them. This narrative can be judiciously supplemented by artistic images of the crucifixion, which help many to focus on the event of Christ's death, and its significance.[42] The apologist may appeal to other literary narratives of sacrificial love to reinforce this Gospel narrative, but they can never replace it. And the imagination having been captured, the theological significance of Christ's death can begin to percolate through the mind, allowing the apologist to begin to interweave the New Testament narratives about Christ with its theological interpretation of his meaning for humanity.

A Parable of the Kingdom: What Do We Really Desire?

Our fourth biblical narrative is a story within the story of Christ—one of the celebrated "parables of the kingdom." Often described in popular literature as "earthly stories with heavenly meanings," the parables might more accurately be seen as expanded analogies that are used to explain or convince their audiences.[43] Their key function is to enable their hearers to see things in a new way, grasping something that was hitherto elusive or making a connection that they had failed to see up to that point. If we are to live in the "kingdom of God," we need to be able to visualize what this looks like and picture ourselves in it. We look *through* the parables to see the new world that they anticipate, forcing us to rethink the nature of our world and our place in it.[44]

The background to the parables is, of course, the rural Judean culture of the first century. Although some parables are more elaborate and extended, focusing on the dynamics of personal relationships (such as the parable of the prodigal son), most take the form of observations on everyday aspects of agrarian life—such as seeds growing, trees failing to fruit, and animals getting lost. The parables are often memorable, precisely because they are so short. The hearers are drawn into the stories, carrying them home with them and turning them over in their minds. In effect, the parables are like seeds, planted in people's minds and capable of germinating in their own good time.

Although the primary role of Christ's parables was to communicate his teaching about the kingdom of God, their vivid imagery offers us important apologetic opportunities today. Using the parables apologetically should be considered an extension of their reach, not a distortion of their purpose. As Jewish scholar David Stern points out, rabbinic parables were often used apologetically.[45] Indeed, there are several points at which parables seem to serve an apologetic function in Christ's teaching.[46] To explore such possibilities, we shall focus on one of the short "parables of the kingdom"— the parable of the pearl of great price:[47] "The kingdom of heaven is like a merchant in search of fine pearls; on finding one pearl of great value, he went and sold all that he had and bought it" (Matt.

13:45–46). The narrative is terse and minimalist, a mere twenty-five words in the original Greek. It sketches the outlines of a story that a preacher must try to fill in imaginatively to add the detail and texture that some audiences might expect. Yet the story has sufficient imaginative capacity to draw us into its world of meaning, even in its unembellished form.

The first point to appreciate is that we lose the imaginative power of this parable (or any parable, for that matter) if we try to reduce it to didactic or moral principles. Parables are narratives, which demand that their genre be respected. A parable is truth enfolded in a narrative, which must be allowed to remain a story rather than being converted into some timeless abstract truth. As C. S. Lewis noted, it is by enjoying and engaging a narrative that "we come nearest to experiencing as a concrete what can otherwise be understood only as an abstraction."[48] Narratives allow us to tell what it is like to *taste* reality, before we attempt to capture it in abstract terms.

So what "concrete" reality might this parable allow us to experience? And how can we use this in apologetics? In what follows, I shall explore one way of reading this parable, which sees it as the quest for fulfillment of the heart's desire. Although traditional philosophical discussion of the rationality of religious belief has tended to focus on intellectual arguments for the existence of God, there are clear signs of a growing recognition of the importance of the theme of *desiring* God and its wider implications.[49] What explanation can be offered for the deep human desire for something of ultimate significance, which is at best only suppressed—and not satisfied—by the objects of this world?

Augustine of Hippo, Blaise Pascal, and C. S. Lewis all argue that since we have been created by God in order to relate to God, there is a *desiderium naturale*—a natural desire within the human heart for God, whether or not this is recognized for what it really is.[50] We may attach this desire to things within the world, which, by failing to satisfy us, disclose that they are not the true object of this yearning and longing. As Lewis remarks, "Nature cannot satisfy the desires she arouses nor answer theological questions nor sanctify us."[51]

So we return to the parable of the pearl of great price. This succinct narrative leaves space for imaginative embellishment. Who is this merchant? Why was he in search of fine pearls? Exactly what did he find in the pearl of great price that led him to sell everything that he had in order to purchase it? And did he live happily ever after?

Let's retell the story. A merchant finds a priceless pearl for sale and decides that he ought to sell everything in order to possess it. Why? Because he has found something that is not merely costly but also supremely worth possessing. In its light, everything he already possesses seems of little value. The pearls he already owns have created and then intensified an appetite for beauty that they have proved incapable of satisfying. The merchant believes they are the goal of his quest; in fact, they turn out to be merely a stage in his search for something of transcendent and permanent value. The good simply makes the merchant yearn for the best—something that he knows he has not yet found. And then he stumbles across that special pearl he has been waiting for.

So what might this narrative mean? What response might this elicit from us? The merchant comes across a special pearl that captivates him, perhaps giving rise to a devastating moment of illumination in which he realizes the inadequacy of what he had once thought to be satisfying. He wants and needs something better, something that will really satisfy him. Seen in this way, the parable engages the long human search for meaning and significance.

The parable thus reminds us that many of the beliefs and values that we take hold of are like those lesser pearls. They seemed worthwhile and for a time offered fulfillment. Yet, deep down, we knew that there had to be something better. As we shall see in the next chapter, many personal narratives of coming to faith—such as those of Augustine of Hippo and C. S. Lewis—arise from a sense of disillusionment and inadequacy, which makes individuals receptive to the hope of a greater good, a bigger picture of reality, which had up to that moment eluded them.

This is a central theme in C. S. Lewis's first published work, *The Pilgrim's Regress* (1933).[52] Its central character is the pilgrim—John—who has visions of an island that evokes a sense of intense yet transitory longing on his part. At times, John is overwhelmed by this sense of yearning, as he struggles to make sense of it. Where does it come from? And just what is he yearning *for*? Lewis follows Pascal's line of thought in answering this question: there is an "abyss" within the human soul that is so deep only God can fill it. Or, to use Lewis's own imagery, there is a "chair" in the human soul, awaiting the arrival of some honored guest: "If nature makes nothing in vain, the One who can sit in this chair must exist."[53]

All other explanations and proposed goals for this sense of yearning seem to fail to satisfy, either intellectually or existentially. They are "false objects" of desire, whose falsity is ultimately exposed by their failure to satisfy the deepest yearnings of humanity.

> If a man diligently followed this desire, pursuing the false objects until their falsity appeared and then resolutely abandoning them, he must at last come into the clear knowledge that the human soul was made to enjoy some object that is never fully given—nay, cannot even be imagined as given—in our present mode of subjective and spatio-temporal experience.[54]

While Lewis's prose makes no explicit reference to the parable of the pearl of great price, the convergence of their conclusions can hardly be overlooked.

This brief discussion will hopefully indicate the considerable apologetic potential of the retelling of the parables of the kingdom.

It is not surprising that many apologists focus on the parable of the prodigal son (Luke 15:11–32), with its central themes of alienation, disconnection, reconciliation, and homecoming—each of which could be the basis of an apologetic conversation. Perhaps the most significant retellings of this parable are found in the works of Marilynne Robinson, especially *Gilead* (2004) and *Home* (2008).[55] These novels are best read in full for enjoyment and apologetic insight, and it would be impossible to do them justice in this brief section. Robinson shows us how biblical narratives might be retold apologetically and leaves the door open for others to follow her example.

In this chapter, we have reflected on how biblical narratives can be used apologetically. Limits of space have restricted both the number of such narratives to be considered and the extent to which we have engaged with them. Yet it is clear, even from this very inadequate discussion, that these narratives possess enormous potential, when rightly used, to capture the human imagination, and create receptivity to a Christian way of thinking and living.

5.

Strategies and Criteria for Narrative Apologetics

The analysis offered in this book suggests that narrative apologetics is a theologically legitimate and culturally appropriate way of engaging the concerns, anxieties, and questions of our age, potentially creating receptivity and attentiveness to the themes of the gospel. Christians must engage the dominant stories of our culture, either by telling a better story that shows that these stories are inadequate or incoherent, or through subversive storytelling in which they enter into a rival cultural narrative and retell its story in light of the Christian worldview.[1] We are called to out-narrate the dominant stories that shape our culture, by exposing their weaknesses or showing how they are enfolded by our own or how they are eclipsed by a more luminous and compelling story.

Strategies for Narrative Apologetics

So how might this be done? There has been much interest in the general question of how literary and cultural narratives can be assessed—for example, their correlation with an external world and their internal coherence.[2] Three broad strategies can be proposed for narrative apologetics, each of which has its own distinct character and virtues. A Christian narrative apologetics will aim to show that Christianity tells a better story than its rivals; that it presents a deeper account of reality, enfolding whatever truths are communicated by other stories; and that it enables rival narratives of reality to be challenged and critiqued. In what follows, we shall consider each of these approaches and reflect on its potential application.

Telling a Better Story

Christian apologetics aims to show the deeper appeal and capaciousness of the Christian story. In his 1941 sermon "The Weight of Glory," C. S. Lewis asks how the cultural dominance of a materialist metanarrative might be broken. Like any ideology, this metanarrative seeks to make not merely the idea that earth is our home but also the idea that there is no transcendent dimension to life seem *normal*. All ideologies aim to achieve invisibility so that their ideas and values are simply assumed to be true. So how can their spell be broken?

Lewis's answer remains significant: *to break a spell, you have to weave a better spell.* "Spells are used for breaking enchantments as well as for inducing them. And you and I have need of the strongest spell that can be found to wake us from the evil enchantment of worldliness that has been laid upon us for nearly a hundred years."[3] To break the spell of one narrative, a better narrative needs to be told, one capable of capturing the imagination and opening the mind to alternative possibilities.

This first approach thus sets out to exhibit the rational, moral, and imaginative vision of the Christian faith. Although a narrative appeals primarily to the imagination, it also allows and encourages connections with human reason and experience. There are ways in which a sensitive presentation of the fundamentals of Christian theology can serve an important apologetic role. Although some argue that the best apologetics is a good systematic theology,[4] this overstatement requires careful nuancing. There is, after all, a significant difference between teaching theology to the committed and commending the spiritual and intellectual vision articulated by theology to outsiders and seekers. Apologetics unquestionably rests upon and draws upon the core themes of systematic theology, yet its *genre* and its *voice* are quite different.

We can draw on the work of social theorist Charles Taylor in developing this point. Taylor persuasively argues that there is a need to move away from the traditional believers-nonbelievers paradigm to a new *seekers-dwellers paradigm*, with important implications for the way in which the church engages its own members and the wider culture.[5] Taylor's analysis of modern secularism suggests that "our options for belief are more numerous, optional and contestable"[6] than ever before, as we find ourselves "caught between myriad options for pursuing meaning, significance and fullness."[7]

This way of thinking, originally developed by American sociologist Robert Wuthnow,[8] highlights the different needs and expectations of those who already inhabit the Christian tradition (and wish to understand and enact it better) and those who are drawn to it from outside but have yet to grasp how it might connect with their hopes and fears. Dogmatics might well speak to at least some "dwellers"; a quite different mode of discourse, however, is required to engage the needs and questions of "seekers."

Developing this point, leading Czech writer Tomáš Halík emphasizes the importance of the "fringe"—the liminal zone at the interface between the church and the world, which prevents that church from becoming a sect rather than a church in the proper sense of the word.[9] The "fringe" is a "zone of questions and doubts,"[10] where a "seeking church" can encounter and engage seekers who are both curious and shy and prefer to remain on the margins of an institution they distrust. The maintenance of this fringe is thus essential to the continuing ministry of the church, not least in providing a space within which those whose original faith has been shaken can arrive at a deeper faith that is at home with paradox and mystery.

In his *Ways of Judgment*, leading British moral theologian Oliver O'Donovan points out that apologetics is "not a distinct genre of religious thinking" but rather is "a distinct genre of *exposition*." The same fundamental ideas lie behind both theology and apologetics; the difference between them lies in the manner in which they are presented, reflecting the different intended audiences. While there are no apologetic reasons and arguments that do not belong within "the ordered exposition of Christian belief," the apologetic needs of the situation may lead me to "organize my account of my beliefs in relation to somebody else's doubts or counter-arguments."[11] "Different trains of theological thought may acquire greater or lesser apologetic weight circumstantially, as the crises or doubts of the culture may dictate at any moment. One train of Christian thought that carries apologetic weight in our times is the capacity of faith to display the intelligibility of political institutions and traditions."[12]

O'Donovan's point is well taken. Apologetic strategies must be attentive to the opportunities of the moment. Current interest in moral and political issues creates the possibility of positive and creative dialogue between Christianity and the wider culture. Yet other such apologetic dialogues are certainly possible and desirable. For O'Donovan, apologetics is not to be *identified* with systematic theology but is a manner of expounding and communicating the core themes of Christian faith that is sensitive to the "crises or doubts" of our cultural contexts. It is the natural outcome of a rich theological foundation, but its modes of communication and commendation are not the same as those of Christian dogmatics.

Apologetics and systematic theology are certainly related and interconnected; they are not, however, the same.

Let us return to C. S. Lewis as we reflect on how a "better story" might be told. In the course of his period as an atheist during the 1920s, Lewis found himself reflecting on the capacity of various worldviews to do justice to the complexity of reality. Modernist writers such as atheists George Bernard Shaw and H. G. Wells seemed to Lewis to be "a little thin"; there was "no depth in them"; they were "too simple." Their cultural metanarratives seemed incapable of adequately representing the "roughness and density of life."[13] Yet Lewis found that Christian poet George Herbert was remarkably successful in "conveying the very quality of life as we actually live it," apparently on account of "mediating" reality through what Lewis then termed "the Christian mythology."[14]

This surprising discovery made Lewis increasingly receptive to considering Christianity as a "big picture" of reality. While it did not lead directly to his conversion, it appears to have made him open to this alternative way of seeing things. For Lewis, this "better" story seemed to be more capable of "conveying the very quality of life as we actually live it" than its atheist alternatives.[15] In his later reflections on the apologetic importance of this point, Lewis noted how a story needs to "chime in" with the human experience of reality if it is to carry weight with an audience and open up new possibilities.

Seeing the Christian Story as a Metanarrative

One of the most significant goals of Christian apologetics is to show that what is good, true, and beautiful can be convincingly accommodated within the Christian narrative. This approach proposes that the Christian story is to be seen not as a local narrative but as a deeper account of things, capable of accommodating valid insights from other narratives, while at the same time positioning them within its own framework. J. R. R. Tolkien did not refer to Christianity as a metanarrative but conveyed essentially the same idea through his more helpful phrase "a story of a larger kind." For Tolkien, this larger story embraced what was good, true, and beautiful in the great stories of human culture and literature, such as Nordic myths.[16]

This second strategy has a long history of use. In his *Three Rival Versions of Moral Enquiry* (1990), Alasdair MacIntyre sets out what he considers to be the three main approaches to moral reflection, such as understanding moral inquiry as being grounded in time-less universal rational principles, which have enabled the rational progress of humanity. MacIntyre regards each of these as flawed and finds these deficiencies to be exposed and corrected by classical Thomism. My concern here, however, is not to evaluate MacIntyre's conclusion but to consider how he reaches it in the first place.

So what criteria does MacIntyre use to make this judgment? How does he defend his view that classical Thomism offers a more compelling and trustworthy tradition of moral inquiry than its three main rivals? His answer is significant: the best narrative prevails over its rivals because it proves "able to include its rivals within it, not only to retell their stories as episodes within its story, but to tell the story of the telling of their stories as such episodes."[17] This renarration of someone else's metanarrative within the broader framework provided by one's own is ultimately an assertion of the greater explanatory capaciousness of one's preferred narrative.

This basic approach is particularly associated with the natural sciences, in which successful grand theories are seen to both incor-porate and contextualize earlier successful theories. The "unifica-tionist" approach to scientific explanation holds that the best theory is able to accommodate all the valid insights of earlier theories, while at the same time expanding their horizons and identifying the basis of its plausibility.[18] This is nicely illustrated by the transition from classical Newtonian mechanics to relativistic quantum mechanics, which took place during the first few decades of the twentieth century.[19]

In the eighteenth and nineteenth centuries, classical mechanics was seen as a self-sufficient and intellectually autonomous area of theory, capable of accounting for what could be observed in nature. Yet following the work of Max Planck, Albert Einstein, and Niels Bohr in the early twentieth century, it was realized that classical mechanics was a special, limiting case of a grander theory. Relativistic quantum mechanics was proposed as a more fundamental theory, capable of far greater explanatory capacity, in that it was able to account for both the successes and the failures of classical mechanics by identifying its limited sphere of validity. The "correspondence principle," first identified by Niels Bohr in 1923, sets out, clearly and elegantly, how quantum mechanics reduces to classical mechanics under certain limits.[20]

Neither relativistic quantum mechanics nor quantum field theory invalidated classical mechanics; they simply demonstrated that it was a special or limiting case of a more comprehensive and complex theory.[21] The classical model was thus accounted for on the basis of the greater explanatory capacity of the relativistic model, and the limits of their correspondence were established. And perhaps more importantly, the relativistic approach explained why the classic theory worked in certain situations and not in others. Its validity was affirmed within certain limits.

Elsewhere, I have suggested that the Christian faith can be thought of as offering a *metarationality*—a greater vision of rationality that is able to accommodate and account for what we might call "everyday human rationality," while at the same time helping us grasp its limits.[22] The distinct trinitarian logic of the Christian faith is the greater framework—a way of understanding ourselves and our world that transcends the limits of human reason yet at the same time helps us position what we might call our "native" or everyday rationality within an informing context. Human rationality operates within limits—and outside those limits, it distorts and impoverishes our understanding of God and our universe.

In the specific case of narrative apologetics, the apologist can aim to show *at least* that the Christian narrative is a meaningful and credible option in today's world, and *if possible* that this narrative is capable of positioning and accounting for other narratives. We have already considered J. R. R. Tolkien's important discussion of this theme; a similar approach was developed by C. S. Lewis, who held that Christianity was not one myth alongside many others but rather represented the fulfillment of all myths—the "true myth" toward which all other myths merely pointed, or "God's myth" from which "human myths" ultimately derived and toward which they ultimately point.[23] Christianity thus tells a true story about humanity that makes sense of all the stories that humanity tells about itself—and provides robust answers to the questions they raise yet tantalizingly fail to answer satisfactorily.

Offering Criticism of Rival Narratives

Narrative apologetics can also be used critically, as a tool for challenging the credibility of the dominant narratives of our culture. This is a preliminary move before proposing the Christian narrative as a better account of reality; the objective here is initially not to commend Christianity but to challenge the integrity and intellectual reliability of an influential alternative narrative and in doing so to remove a roadblock to the serious consideration of the gospel. If this dominant narrative proves unreliable, what alternatives might be considered?

One of the most obvious applications of this approach relates to the "conflict narrative" of the relation of science and religion, which has been adopted by writers such as Richard Dawkins and Christopher Hitchens as emblematic of the New Atheism.[24] The "conflict narrative" is a highly eclectic reading of Western cultural history that holds that there is a perennial and essential conflict between science and religion. Dawkins intensifies this image, speaking of the *warfare* of science and faith and asserting that this entails the notion that any scientist with religious beliefs is a traitor to science. Scientists are thus intellectually prohibited from holding religious beliefs, in that this amounts to appeasement or treason.[25]

Apart from being a hysterical overstatement of the situation, this represents an unacceptably selective and biased reading of history. J. A. Froude, a former Regius Professor of Modern History at Oxford University, was withering in his criticism of such cherry-picking approaches to history: "It often seems to me as if history is like a child's box of letters, with which we can spell any word we please. We have only to pick out such letters as we want, arrange them as we like, and say nothing about those which do not suit our purpose."[26]

The serious deficiencies of such polemical readings of history are easily demonstrated from Christopher Hitchens's *God Is Not Great* (2007), a flagship manifesto of the New Atheism. Noting (correctly) that Christian writer Timothy Dwight (1752–1811) opposed smallpox vaccination,[27] Hitchens draws the wider conclusion that Dwight's position demonstrates how religious obscurantism stood in the way of scientific advance then, as it continues to do to this day. Religion poisons all attempts at human progress. The specific example confirms the general principle.

But Hitchens's simplistic narrative is both subverted and redirected through a closer reading of the history of smallpox inoculation. For example, Jonathan Edwards (1703–58)—now widely regarded as America's greatest religious thinker—was a strong supporter of scientific advance and was committed to the new medical procedure of smallpox inoculation using the "variolation" technique introduced into America from Europe by Cotton Mather (1663–1728), probably the most famous Puritan pastor in New England.[28] Wanting to reassure his students at Princeton that it was safe, Edwards was vaccinated himself—only to die as a result.[29] Using the same highly selective narrative approach favored by Hitchens, it could be argued that this single case proves that Christianity was supportive of scientific advance.

Or, to complexify Hitchens's inadequate and superficial account still further, consider the case of the atheist writer George Bernard Shaw (1856–1950), who opposed smallpox vaccination in the 1930s, ridiculing it as a "delusion." He dismissed leading scientists whose research supported it—such as Louis Pasteur and Joseph Lister—as charlatans who knew nothing about the scientific method.[30] Applying Hitchens's cherry-picking approach, it could be argued that this single case provides that atheism was hostile toward scientific advance.

But nobody with any knowledge of the history of smallpox vaccination and concerned to tell its full story would draw such ludicrous conclusions. History is complex. It is open to multiple interpretations, none of which is self-evidently "right." Revisionist approaches to many of the historical incidents traditionally interpreted in light of the "conflict" or "warfare" narrative have debunked these interpretations.[31] Their continued use within the New Atheist movement is a worrying indication that it relies upon "fake news" for its intellectual and cultural appeal. As philosopher John Gray points out, the New Atheism is precariously dependent upon what is little more than "a tedious re-run of a Victorian squabble between science and religion."[32]

The origins of the "conflict narrative" lie specifically in the social world of the final quarter of the nineteenth century, when it emerged as a polemical strategy to ensure the independence of the natural sciences from ecclesiastical control.[33] Other narratives—such as that of the potential enrichment of science and faith—can be proposed that are far more sensitive to the historical evidence than those of the "conflict" model.[34] The New Atheism's decision to allow itself to become dependent on the "conflict" narrative must now be seen as unwise, leaving it exposed to potentially lethal criticism as historical research continues to erode its intellectual foundations.

Thus far, we have outlined three broad strategies for narrative apologetics. Yet these strategies themselves open up further questions—above all, how we might go about deciding which is the "best" narrative. We shall consider this in the next section.

Criteria of Relevance for Narrative Apologetics

Humans are storytellers and story-dwellers. Some stories are received, some are discovered, and some are simply invented. C. S. Lewis's Chronicles of Narnia are fundamentally about discovering a story that makes sense of all other stories—and then embracing it, because of its power to give meaning and value to life. But which is the true story? Which are merely its shadows and echoes? And which are fabrications, tales spun to entrap and deceive?

At an early stage in *The Lion, the Witch and the Wardrobe*, the four Pevensie children begin to hear stories about the true origins and destiny of Narnia. Puzzled, they find they have to make decisions about which persons and which stories are to be trusted. Is Narnia really the realm of the White Witch? Or is she a usurper, whose power will be broken when two Sons of Adam and two Daughters of Eve sit on the four thrones at Cair Paravel? Is Narnia really the realm of the mysterious Aslan, whose return is expected at any time? As the children realize, they need to work out how stories are to be tested.

Gradually, one narrative emerges as supremely plausible: the story of the noble lion, Aslan. Each individual story of Narnia turns out to be part of this greater narrative. *The Lion, the Witch and the Wardrobe* hints at (and partially discloses) the "big picture," expanded in the remainder of the Narnia volumes. This "grand narrative" of interlocking stories makes sense of the riddles of what the children see and experience around them. It allows the children to understand their experiences with a new clarity and depth, like a camera lens bringing a landscape into sharp focus. In *Mere Christianity*, Lewis helps us to understand Christian ideas; his Chronicles of Narnia, however, allow us to step inside and experience the Christian story, judge it by its ability to make sense of things, and "chime in" with our deepest intuitions about truth, beauty, and goodness.[35]

In his book *Moral, Believing Animals* (2003), Smith identifies the contemporary metanarratives that he believes shape the thinking of Western people—the Christian metanarrative, the Militant Islamic Resurgence narrative, the American Experiment narrative, the Capitalist Prosperity narrative, the Progressive Socialism narrative, the Scientific Enlightenment narrative, the Expressive Romantic narrative, the Destined Unity with Brahman narrative, the Liberal Progress narrative, the Ubiquitous Egoism narrative, and the Chance and Purposelessness narrative.[36]

So which of these many stories about our world and ourselves should we choose? How do we know whether it is truthful and reliable? Which "grand story" allows the best rendering of our complex universe? Which metanarrative offers the most illumination of our shadowy world? And what criteria might be used to make these judgments in the first place? A narrative apologetics cannot avoid such questions—nor should it. Christian apologetics focuses on the question of the trustworthiness of the Christian story and its capacity to illuminate and then to transform our lives.

As a former natural scientist, I have long been interested in the criteria used in choosing scientific theories. The dominant approach to the development of scientific theories is currently known as "inference to the best explanation."[37] A number of theories can always be developed to explain a set of observations. The challenge faced by natural scientists is to determine which of these candidates represents the best explanation.

A number of criteria are often put forward as hallmarks of successful theories, such as simplicity, elegance or beauty, and coherence.[38] Yet these criteria are at best indications of theoretical success. The criteria emerge from scientific practice and are not grounded on a priori metaphysical ideas that are somehow built into the order of things. The best explanation is not always the simplest, and beautiful theories are not always correct. Yet these criteria serve a useful function, in that they allow us to identify the strengths and weaknesses of theories—even if this does not always lead to a secure conclusion about which theory is indeed the best.

So how might we go about judging the stories that lie at the heart of our lives and cultures? How do we evaluate their trustworthiness? We noted earlier the findings of sociologist Christian Smith, who observed that a dozen "grand stories" are regularly used by people in Western culture to make sense of the world and their lives. Smith stresses the importance of these narratives in generating and sustaining a person's meaning. Humans are "animals who make stories but also animals who are *made* by our stories."[39] Furthermore, we tend to use different stories to engage and illuminate different aspects of our lives. A modern American might use a Christian narrative to illuminate and inform some aspects of her life yet draw on the Capitalist Prosperity narrative for others. This entanglement of informing and interpreting narratives is something that can never be entirely resolved or rationalized.

Smith's studies of how people use narratives help us grasp an important point: it is not necessary to show that Christianity offers an exclusive account of reality. The apologist needs to show that the Christian story connects with the deepest questions, concerns, and needs of humanity. People may—and do—draw on other narratives to make sense of some areas of their lives. The Christian narrative illuminates deep questions of meaning and value, offering transformation and renewal in the face of God. Yet it might not answer questions concerning political and social issues, so people might draw on other narratives to help them engage these matters. As we noted earlier (see "The Story of the Exodus: The Hope of Deliverance" in chap. 4), the complexity of human life is such that we need to draw on multiple narratives and multiple maps to deal with its many facets.

These reflections, though helpful, do not resolve the issue of how we decide which narrative is the "best." Smith is clear that this poses some serious and possibly insurmountable problems. "The problem with a narratological understanding of human persons—and probably an important reason modern people resist thinking of themselves as ultimately storytelling and believing and incarnating animals—is that it is difficult rationally to adjudicate between divergent stories. How do you tell which one is more deserving of assent and commitment than others?"[40]

Yet while this is indeed a difficult question to answer, it is important apologetically. At the very least, Christianity must be able to show that its informing and grounding narrative is plausible and capable of engaging meaningfully with at least some major questions of life. So what criteria might be used? In what follows, I shall suggest three basic criteria that seem to be important to people as they engage and assess competing narratives, and reflect on the apologetic significance of these criteria.

Offering a Realistic Account of Our World

Some say we are entering a post-truth era, in which we simply make up our beliefs to suit our personal taste. We create a world that fits with our preconceived ideas or our deepest longings and take offense when our imagined certainties are challenged. Why worry about someone else's so-called reality, when we can create our own and thus make our beliefs serve our longings? For some in this post-truth world, a metanarrative is nothing more than a convenient fiction, created to serve our wishes. Earlier, we noted how Thomas Nagel's atheism is a post hoc rationalization of his fundamental longing for a godless world (see "Meeting Objections: God as a Projection" in chap. 3).

This does not, of course, in any way preclude a fictional narrative from making important moral points or illuminating significant intellectual issues. Stanley Hauerwas points out that while *Watership Down* (1972) was clearly a fictional work about rabbits, it nevertheless made some powerful and valid points about the importance of transmitting stories and how the loss of a defining narrative leads to the fragmentation and dissolution of a community.[41] Yet the truth of these insights is neither established nor guaranteed by the story line of *Watership Down*. If these Leporidian insights are indeed true, then their truthfulness must be established on other grounds, so that the novel *illustrates* them, without actually *validating* them. *Watership Down* thus highlights the need to determine whether a given narrative is able to both produce and confirm ideas or values.

The Christian narrative is both *generative* and *validating*. In other words, distinctively Christian ideas and values arise from a dramatic narrative of creation, redemption, and consummation and find their grounds of authorization and justification from within that narrative itself.[42] This important insight resonates with both recent narrative approaches to theology, noted earlier (see "Why Stories Matter" in chap. 1), and traditional evangelical approaches that emphasize the Bible itself as a source of ideas and values.[43] As is often stressed, the Bible is firmly rooted in history, on the one hand, while offering an interpretation of that history that transcends any specific time or place, on the other.

At times, the Christian theological tradition has amplified those ideas by establishing interconnections not necessarily found within—though not for that reason inconsistent with—the core biblical narrative; at times, it may even, whether by accident or design, have assimilated them into ideas deriving from other sources, potentially distorting the biblical dynamic. For example, N. T. Wright has argued that some Protestants have *moralized* the core problem of humanity (seeing sin essentially as violations of an ethical or cultural code), *paganized* the solution to this problem (by suggesting that an angry Father takes out his anger on his Son), and *Platonized* the goal of the Christian life (by thinking of going to heaven when we die, rather than focusing on the core notion of resurrection).[44] All these points are open for discussion within the community of faith, yet the very possibility of that discussion itself illustrates that the Christian narrative has the capacity for self-correction when needed.

Creating Space for the Reader

The best narratives arguably create space for their readers to step inside them, seeing themselves described or analyzed in the text. A good example of this lies in Charles Colson's conversion to Christianity in the aftermath of the Watergate scandal. During a visit with Colson in August 1973, Tom Phillips—then chairman of the Raytheon Corporation—read aloud to him the chapter titled "The Great Sin" from C. S. Lewis's *Mere Christianity*.[45] Colson recognized himself in the text, which both diagnosed his problem and pointed toward its cure. The trustworthiness of the diagnosis opened him to embrace its capacity to cure.

It is no accident that many readers of the Gospel narratives find themselves drawn to the accounts of encounters of Jesus Christ with individuals—such as Nicodemus (John 3:1–21), Zacchaeus (Luke 19:2–10), or the anonymous woman at the well (John 4:7–26). The passages are not about the enunciation of generic ideas directed toward anyone who happens to be around but rather are about specific engagements that reflect the individuality of the person whom Christ encounters.

The critical point is that the Christian narrative needs to speak to *us individually*, not merely to *someone else*. We need to feel—or to be helped to realize—that we are being addressed and engaged. We need to be able to see ourselves in that story. This points to the importance of the core Christian narrative itself and also helps clarify the role of its apologetic interpreters. Their task is to construct a bridge from the narrative to its audience—whether that audience is a single individual or a group of people. This, it must be stressed, is about *exhibiting the intrinsic significance* of the Christian narrative, not about *imposing an external constructed significance* upon that narrative.

It is abundantly clear that the Christian narrative, when properly interpreted, has an intrinsic capacity to engage all kinds of human situations. Yet it is the task of the interpreter of that narrative to translate and transpose it, with the specific situation of the audience in mind.[46] We have already noted the importance of this point in speaking of the "love of God" (see "The Story of Jesus Christ: Rendering the Love of God" in chap. 4); it is instructive to consider how this could also be applied to other core Christian ideas.

Making Sense of Our Existence

Finally, we can judge the relevance of a story in terms of its ability to make sense of the world in which we live and our own personal existence. Narratives serve an important role in that they can connect otherwise disconnected events and show how they belong

113

together in a larger vision of things. We have already considered the importance of narratives in helping people cope with emotional and spiritual trauma in times of distress, partly because they help us cope with events by finding meaning within them.[47] The philosopher Iris Murdoch also noted the "calming" and "whole-making" effect of ways of looking at the world that allow it to be seen as ultimately rational and meaningful.[48] Yet although she expresses this idea of generating a comprehensive vision of the world in her more philosophical writings, the importance of the theme is best seen in her novels, in which she uses narrative to help her readers grasp the importance of this point *imaginatively*, and not merely *rationally*.[49]

The most familiar literary genre that engages this theme of making sense of our world is, of course, crime fiction. In his essay "The Slaughterhouse of Literature,"[50] Franco Moretti reflects on why the works of Sir Arthur Conan Doyle—creator of the London detective Sherlock Holmes—remain so widely read, when other Victorian crime authors are overlooked or neglected. His answer is significant, and of obvious apologetic importance. Conan Doyle makes systematic use of *clues*: entities or observations that demand an explanation that can only be provided by a coherent narrative that binds them together. Some other authors of this period mention clues but seem to have little idea about what to do with them; others make virtually no use of them at all.

Clues are pointers to a larger picture—to a coherent story that can be told, explaining how those clues came into being and what their place and significance is within that story. This point is highlighted by the novelist Dorothy L. Sayers, who emphasizes the need for a coherent narrative to provide connections between clues.[51] Sayers sees human beings as searching for "patterns" in life,[52] and she explores this theme in her Peter Wimsey detective novels as well as her religious writings. How can we find the best explanation of what we observe? What is the best story that we can tell, that holds as many of these clues together as persuasively as possible? Sayers's point is echoed by Michael Goldberg, who emphasizes the need for a "narrative which can bind the facts of our experience together into a coherent pattern" and thus allow our ideas and lives to "gain their full intelligibility."[53]

Sayers argues that the success of detective fiction is based on our deep yearning to make sense of things, above all to connect together what may initially seem to be an unrelated series of events. Sayers makes her point by appealing to the Greek legend of Theseus and the Minotaur. Theseus is challenged to enter the dark and complex Cretan labyrinth, kill the Minotaur, and find his way out again. His lover, Ariadne, gives him a ball of thread, so that he can leave a trail behind him that he can follow afterward and thus escape from the labyrinth. For Sayers, detective novels are about finding a narrative thread that connects events and holds them together. We "follow, step by step, Ariadne's thread, and finally arrive at the centre of the labyrinth."[54] Sayers later spoke of the intellectual "satisfaction of plaiting and weaving together innumerable threads to make a pattern, a tapestry, a created beauty."[55]

Sayers held that the Christian narrative is *dramatic*, making a deep appeal to the imagination. Yet it also discloses patterns by which we can "make sense of the universe," disclosing its otherwise hidden patterns and finding meaning within its mysteries. Some have suggested that her novel *The Nine Tailors* addresses the "mystery of the universe," while *Gaudy Night* engages the "mystery of the human heart."[56]

As Sayers discovered, Christianity offers a dramatic narrative that helped her make sense of her world. Always self-critical, she at times wondered if she had fallen in love with the intellectual pattern that Christianity disclosed, rather than with the central character of that narrative. Yet Sayers knew the importance of discerning that pattern and knowing that there was some deeper unity and coherence within the world. Sayers here echoes the New Testament itself, which speaks of all things "holding together" or being "knit together" in Christ (Col. 1:17).

Thus far, we have focused on the question of intelligibility and coherence, exploring the ways in which the Christian narrative helps us make sense of our world and ourselves and helps us discern the fundamental interconnectedness of reality. Though these are important, many would argue that the most important human concern is finding meaning in life. This rich and important theme, already hinted at in this chapter, is of such importance that it demands a fuller treatment in its own right, which we will turn to in the next chapter.

6.

The Christian Story and the Meaning of Life

We cannot simply eat, sleep, hunt and reproduce—we are meaning-seeking creatures. . . . We seem to need some higher purpose, some point to our lives—money and leisure, social progress, are just not enough.

Jeanette Winterson[1]

In her personal memoirs, the novelist Jeanette Winterson highlights her growing recognition of the significance of the human quest for meaning and its impact on our existence. Human beings actively seek systems of meaning that embrace an understanding of the world, our personal significance, and our capacity to transcend our limits and locations, as we sense we are part of something bigger and greater. And as we have already seen, narratives are ideally suited to explore these deep questions of meaning, not least by telling the story of how individuals find meaning in life and the difference that this makes in the way they think and live.

Empirical research on how people express and apply the idea of meaning suggests that it is helpful to draw a distinction between "global" and "situational" meaning.[2] *Global* meaning systems weave together beliefs, goals, and subjective feelings of meaning or purpose in life to give a "big picture" of reality. Yet we use this overarching global framework of beliefs, goals, and sense of purpose to structure our lives and to assign meanings to specific experiences—in other words, to determine *situational* meaning.

The "big picture" thus frames our experiences and helps us work out what they mean. It is not difficult to see how this allows us to think of the Christian metanarrative as "global," with "situational" or "local" applications. One person might apply this "global" framework to her own situation and come up with a "local" meaning that might be quite different from what someone else might develop—even though both had adopted the same "global" meaning. Why? Because our individual lives and circumstances are different.

A metanarrative that cannot engage the specifics of an individual's situation will always seem distant and impersonal, in that it cannot secure traction on a person's deepest cares and concerns. One of the most remarkable features of the Gospel accounts of Christ's encounters with individuals is that he relates to them in their irreducible individuality—a theme that is echoed at many points in the Christian metanarrative itself.

So why is the question of meaning so important to human beings? Social psychologist Erich Fromm was shocked by the insanity and destructiveness of the First World War and wondered how individuals could cope with inhabiting such a senseless world. How could anyone find meaning within this apparent meaninglessness? His answer lay in developing what he called a "framework of orientation and devotion," a way of thinking about the world that endows human existence with purpose and significance.[3] Although Fromm developed his own specific framework for coping with this baffling world, what is more important is his recognition that we need such frameworks if we are to live and act in the world without going insane. Living purposefully and meaningfully requires a conceptual frame of reference, a mental map that offers us a secure foundation and focus for our lives.

These insights were further developed by the Austrian neurologist and psychiatrist Viktor Frankl, whose experiences in Nazi concentration camps during the Second World War led him to realize the importance of discerning meaning if we are to cope with traumatic situations.[4] Whether people survived depended on their will to live, which in turn depended on being able to find meaning and purpose in even the most demoralizing situations, which would otherwise be experienced as overwhelmingly destructive. Those who coped best were those who had frameworks of meaning that enabled them to frame their traumatic experiences within their core narratives. The Christian narrative of a suffering savior resonated deeply with the human experience of suffering, enabling people to cope with adversity and even to grow through it—a well-recognized phenomenon now widely referred to as "post-traumatic growth."[5]

In this chapter, we shall explore how the Christian metanarrative establishes meaning and how this opens up important apologetic opportunities and approaches. We begin our reflections by considering the distinction between how things *function* and what things *mean*.

Meaning and Function: A Crucial Distinction

There is a critically important distinction between understanding *how things work* and grasping *what they mean*. Meaning is quite distinct from functionality. The natural sciences are excellent, even outstanding, in helping us discern how things work; indeed, they might even help us to figure out how they might work better. Yet the deeper questions of meaning and value—what Karl Popper termed "ultimate questions"[6]—lie beyond the reach of the methods of the natural sciences. Spanish philosopher José Ortega argued that human flourishing and well-being require more than the partial account of reality that science offers.[7] We need a "big picture," an "integral idea of the universe" that possesses existential depth, and not merely cognitive functionality.

Peter Medawar, who won the Nobel Prize for Medicine for his work on immunology, observes that "only humans find their way by a light that illuminates more than the patch of ground they stand on."[8] Human beings seem to possess some desire to reach beyond the mechanics of engagement with our world, looking for deeper patterns of significance and meaning. Yet for Medawar, science could not answer questions about human meaning, value, or purpose. These questions lie outside, and would always lie outside, the scope of the natural sciences. To expect science to be able to answer ultimate questions is on the same level as expecting Euclid's axioms and postulates to teach us how to bake a cake.[9]

As the philosopher Nicholas Rescher has remarked, human knowledge of the "value dimension of experience" by which we judge certain things to be "beautiful or delightful or tragic" remains outside the range of science.[10] These are not empirical questions that can be answered by the natural sciences.

In his 1990 Herbert Read Memorial Lecture at Cambridge University, Salman Rushdie argued that religion has met three types of needs that have not been satisfied by secular, rationalist materialism. First, it enables us to articulate our sense of awe and wonder, partly by helping us grasp the immensity of life and partly by affirming that we are special. Second, it provides "answers to the unanswerable," engaging the deep questions that so often trouble and perplex us. And finally, it offers us a moral framework within which we can live out the good life. For Rushdie, religion or the "idea of God" provides us with a "repository of our awestruck wonderment at life, and an answer to the great questions of existence." Any attempt to describe or define human beings "in terms that exclude their spiritual needs" will only end in failure.[11]

Rushdie's analysis naturally leads us to ask what sort of "answers to the unanswerable" he had in mind. If the natural sciences cannot answer our deepest questions about meaning, value, and purpose through the legitimate use of its methods, how can we answer them at all? The simple answer is this: by not depending on the natural sciences for such answers, but by looking toward other sources of meaning—above all, to Christianity, which sets out a "big picture" of reality, which provides a framework for engaging the ideas of truth, beauty, and goodness. The philosopher Keith Yandell highlights this aspect of faith: "A religion is a conceptual system that provides an interpretation of the world and the place of human beings in it, bases an account of how life should be lived given that interpretation, and expresses this interpretation and lifestyle in a set of rituals, institutions and practices."[12]

Difficulties in defining "religion"—for example, the existence of "atheist religions" such as Buddhism[13]—have led some scholars to suggest that the notion of a "worldview" is less problematic and potentially more illuminating.[14] Christianity itself can be presented as a worldview,[15] at least in some respects, although it clearly cannot be *reduced* to this category. A worldview can be understood as a complex set of representations concerning issues of meaning and understanding in relation to "big questions" such as ontology, epistemology, and cosmology.[16] It weaves together a number of themes, gaining its distinct character through both the themes that it incorporates and the manner in which it achieves this. As psychologist Mark Koltko-Rivera observes, "A worldview is a way of describing the universe and life within it, both in terms of what is and what ought to be. . . . Worldviews include assumptions that may be unproven, and even unprovable, but these assumptions are superordinate, in that they provide the epistemic and ontological foundations for other beliefs within a belief system."[17]

Worldviews that generate meaning are, of course, found beyond what is normally considered to be a religion—for example, in Marxism or in the metaphysically inflated "universal Darwinism" of Richard Dawkins.[18] As the philosopher Mary Midgley has pointed out, this helps us to understand why Marxism and Darwinism—the "two great secular faiths of our day"—display "religious-looking features."[19]

Yet while the creation or disclosure of meaning may not be a *distinguishing* feature of religion, setting it apart from everything else, it can certainly be argued that it is *characteristic* of it. The stories that individual Christians tell about their lives often focus on questions of meaning. This observation is so important that it needs further consideration.

Personal Narratives: The Embodiment of Meaning

Personal narratives of faith are a testimony to the capacity of the Christian gospel to change people, becoming an important part of their lives, so that an objective truth becomes a subjective reality without losing its objective character. These narratives might take the form of the discovery of the Christian faith or the experience of the capacity of this faith to inspire, console, or sustain in times of struggle and despair. While audiences will find these stories interesting, the most important point is that these stories illustrate and confirm the ability of the Christian faith to become part of someone's life, providing the person hope and meaning.

There are many such narratives, yet all share a common feature: for Christians to tell their own story is for them to speak of how Christianity became real to them as living human beings. It is an affirmation of the truth of faith in the sense of demonstrating its capacity to change life, to give direction and meaning to real people, and to become a transforming reality in an individual's personal existence. There is ample empirical evidence pointing to the importance of personal narratives as a means of connecting an individual's life story with a wider frame of reference and hence discovering meaning and significance.[20]

We can speak of individual Christians embodying meaning. The idea of "embodied meaning" needs a little explanation. It refers to the idea that the way in which a Christian thinks and acts reflects the core themes of the gospel. Instead of thinking of the idea of "meaning" abstractly, we think of it in terms of a lived-out life—what someone does, which expresses and enacts his understanding of what life is all about. We have already looked at one good example of this: the way in which Christians cope with hardship, suffering, and trauma, seeing the story of Jesus Christ as something that they can use as both an example and an inspiration.[21] In telling how they cope with suffering, Christians are thus retelling an important element of the Christian narrative and displaying its impact through their lives.

These personal narratives can be institutionalized. A good example of this lies to hand in the "conversion narratives" that were a requirement for admission to Puritan congregations in New England and elsewhere in the seventeenth century.[22] These narratives were intended to give the congregation a convincing testimony of a person's experience of conversion and the subsequent workings of grace in the person's life. John Rogers (ca. 1570–1636), the Puritan minister of Dedham, required everyone who was to be admitted to his congregation to give oral testimony to "some experimental Evidences of the work of grace upon his soul."[23] One of the functions of these narratives was to demonstrate that Christianity was a living reality in the lives of such individuals, rather than some form of notional assent to a set of doctrines.

These observations make clear the apologetic importance of personal testimony. Believers can speak of how they discovered Christianity, how it became real to them, and the difference that it made. They can speak of their inhabitation of faith and how they learned to cope with doubt and uncertainty, develop their moral values, and face difficulties and troubles. In doing so, they are witnessing to the capacity of faith to generate meaning and sustain people in times of need.

The Christian Narrative and the Disclosure of Meaning

As I have argued throughout this work, Christianity is fundamentally a historically rooted interpretative and transforming narrative that gives rise to a system of concepts and values that provide an integrated framework of meaning in life. It establishes connections between God, Christ, and believers that are woven together within a coherent worldview. Substantial research literature points to the importance of finding meaning for human well-being and also illuminates the role played by religious faith in providing a comprehensive and integrated framework of meaning that helps individuals to transcend their own concerns or experience and connect with something greater.[24] Christians, of course, have always appreciated that their faith enables them to live life meaningfully and authentically; recent psychological studies, in confirming this point, have also helped unfold the various ways in which we understand this core concept of "meaning."

Social psychologist Roy Baumeister set out an influential evidence-based analysis of theories of the meaning of life, in which he identified the themes that had to be engaged and explored before the human quest for meaning could be satisfied.[25] There were, he argued, four fundamental questions that had to be answered convincingly if a worldview was to count as offering a credible account of the "meaning of life":

1. *Identity*: Who am I?
2. *Value*: Do I matter?
3. *Purpose*: Why am I here?
4. *Agency*: Can I make a difference?

Baumeister was clear that psychology could not provide normative answers to these four questions. Questions of meaning appear to lie tantalizing beyond the intellectual horizons and methodological frontiers of the natural sciences. *Yet this does not mean that these questions cannot be answered.* There are other tools we can use in our search for meaningful answers—including the Christian story.

So how does this Christian "grand narrative" engage with these four fundamental questions? In what follows, we shall reflect on each of these questions, outlining some potential apologetic approaches that emerge from them that can be developed and applied further.

Identity: Who Am I?

It is very easy to give definitions of human identity. We are partly defined by our genetic makeup, by our social location, and by countless other scientific parameters. We can be defined with reference to our race, our nationality, our weight, and our gender. Yet all too often this leads to our identity being reduced to genetic and social stereotypes, so that individual identity has become a matter of an impersonal genetic code.

Many have protested against this depersonalization of human identity. Jewish philosopher Martin Buber (1878–1965) has argued that purely scientific accounts of humanity reduce people to objects—to an "it" rather than a "you." It is the "sublime melancholy of our lot that every You must become an It in our world."[26] The essence of personal identity, for Buber, is an ability to exist in relationships. We are defined not by our chemical or genetic makeup but by our social and personal relationships.[27] For Christianity, we are given a new identity as a person of significance by the God who has created and redeemed us and called us by name. We are invited to allow our personal narrative to become part of the greater narrative of God.

We have already noted (see "H. Richard Niebuhr on the Retrieval of Narrative" in chap. 2) the importance of H. Richard Niebuhr's 1941 essay "The Story of Our Lives," which argues that Christians should focus on the "irreplaceable and untranslatable" narrative of faith that straddles the borderlands of history, parable, and myth. This story is not an argument for the existence of God but rather a simple recital of the events surrounding Jesus Christ and an invitation to become part of that story. How participants understand being part of such a shared history is not framed in terms of a detached scientific explanation of life but rather involves a subjective, committed, and engaged attitude to existence, resting on a set of implicit assumptions that need to be unpacked and given systematic formulation.

Niebuhr's essay sees a new interest emerge in the capacity of the Christian story to generate moral values and frameworks of meaning. Writers such as Stanley Hauerwas have explored how this narrative recognizes human brokenness and the need for forgiveness and thus acts as the context of corporate and individual formation, inviting Christians to align and connect the stories of their lives—in terms of both their habits of thought and their actions—with the narrative of the Christian tradition.[28] C. S. Lewis has offered an accessible way of visualizing this point in his Chronicles of Narnia, showing how individual characters in the drama allow their personal narratives to become part of the greater story of Narnia itself—a story that they simultaneously inhabit and advance. Their individual identity and value remain; they realize, however, that they have become part of something grander, which motivates and informs their lives and actions.

Identity, however, is social as much as individual. In recent years, there has been much interest in how biblical narratives shape and inform both individual and communal identities. The role of narratives in shaping ancient Israelite identity is becoming increasingly clear, as scholars have used tools such as social identity theory to clarify how such narratives are intertwined with questions of identity.[29] Yet such biblical narratives can also help shape personal and social identity in the present. A particularly good exploration of this issue is provided by Athena Gorospe's exploration of how the narrative of Moses's return to Egypt (Exod. 4:18–26) can illuminate the social identity of Filipino overseas workers in an age of global economic migration.[30] Gorospe appeals to Paul Ricoeur's hermeneutics of threefold mimesis (prefiguration, configuration, and refiguration) to allow the text to connect with contemporary concerns.

The apologist is thus presented with the task of making connections between the Christian story and the audience, aiming to show how the gospel has the capacity to help us discover who we are and who we are meant to be. It is here that apologetics becomes an art, rather than a science, as it requires a series of gifts—such as empathy and imagination—to help others see how the Christian story connects with, and eventually transforms, their own personal stories.

Value: Do I Matter?

In his "Late Fragment," American poet Raymond Carver speaks movingly of the longing "to know myself beloved, to feel myself beloved on the earth."[31] It is a very human (and very natural) yearning, which helps us appreciate why so many regard personal relationships as being of such significance and find their sense of self-worth affirmed and validated through them. Yet it is a thought that is constantly subverted by reflecting on the apparent insignificance of humanity, when seen in its broader cosmic context.

Sigmund Freud famously argued that scientific advance has led to a radical reevaluation of the place and significance of humanity in the universe, deflating human pretensions to grandeur and uniqueness.[32] Before Copernicus, we thought we stood at the center of all things. Before Darwin, we thought we were utterly distinct from every other living species. Before Freud, we thought that we were masters of our own limited realm; now we have to come to terms with being the prisoner of hidden unconscious forces, subtly influencing our thinking and behavior. And as our knowledge of our universe expands, we realize how many galaxies lie beyond our own. The human lifespan is insignificant in comparison with the immense age of the universe. We can easily be overwhelmed by a sense of our own insignificance when we see ourselves against this vast cosmic backdrop.

This sense of unease is compounded for some by the dominant Western cultural narratives—such as what Christian Smith dubs the Scientific Enlightenment narrative or the Chance and Purposelessness narrative (see "Why Stories Matter" in chap. 1). These portray human beings as simply assemblies of molecules or biological components, devoid of purpose or meaning. This highly reductive approach is found in the writings of biologist Francis Crick, who defined human beings in purely neurological terms. "'You,' your joys and your sorrows, your memories and your ambitions, your sense of personal identity and free will, are in fact no more than the behaviour of a vast assembly of nerve cells and their associated molecules. . . . You're nothing but a pack of neurons."[33] Yet Crick's highly reductive approach to our human identity assumes that a complex system is no more than the sum of its parts—and that one of these components can be singled out as being of supreme importance. Crick's bold overstatement is probably best seen as a neurologist's perspective on human nature, which overlooks the obvious fact that there is a lot more to human nature than neurons. We need neurons to function, but we are not defined exclusively or characteristically in this way.

Others find themselves perplexed by reductive evolutionary narratives of human nature, such as Richard Dawkins's "gene's eye" view of human nature, set out in his landmark book *The Selfish Gene* (1976). This approach, which attracted a lot of attention back in the 1980s, although it has since fallen out of favor,[34] sees human beings essentially as machines that are controlled and determined by their DNA—the complex biological molecule that transmits genetic information. According to Dawkins, "DNA neither cares nor knows. DNA just is. And we dance to its music."[35] Our sole purpose in existing is to pass on our genes to future generations. Human beings are just gene-perpetuating machines.[36]

Dawkins himself has misgivings about this narrative, which holds that we are trapped in patterns of thought and action that are ultimately not of our own choosing. He thus proposes a counternarrative, arguing that we are able to assert our autonomy in the face of this genetic determinism. We can rebel against our selfish genes. "We have the power to defy the selfish genes of our birth. . . . We, alone on earth, can rebel against the tyranny of the selfish replicators."[37] Yet this bold narrative of human autonomy remains located, not entirely consistently, within a narrative of humans as gene machines who are constrained to dance to the music of DNA. Dawkins thus frequently refers to human beings as robots that are programmed to execute the instructions of their genetic masters.

So is our self-worth subverted, if not destroyed, by these reflections? Some would argue that we need to face up to our situation, whether in a bold act of intellectual defiance or a gracious resignation to a bleak emptiness as we contemplate our limited role in the greater scheme of things. Yet the Christian narrative allows us to frame these questions in a very different way than that offered by a bleak secular humanism. By allowing their personal narratives to be embraced and enfolded by the greater narrative of God, Christians see things in a new way—including their own status and identity. We are no longer mere assemblies of molecules, neurons, or genes; we are individuals who can relate to God, and whose status is transformed by God's love and attentiveness toward us.

Christian writers thus speak of the transvaluation of human life through faith. One particularly good example of this is the notion of being "touched" by God, explored in the writings of English poet-theologian George Herbert. Herbert likens the graceful "touch" of God to the fabled "philosopher's stone" of medieval alchemy, which transmutes base metal into gold:

> This is that famous stone
> That turneth all to gold:
> For that which God doth touch and own
> Cannot for less be told.[38]

Through inhabiting the Christian narrative, we come to see ourselves, as medieval writer Julian of Norwich famously put it, as being enfolded in the love of Christ,[39] which brings us a new security, identity, and value. Our self-worth is grounded in being loved by God.

God is one who relates to us and thence transforms our sense of value and significance precisely through this privilege of relationship. We matter to God. One of the most profound pieces of writing in the Old Testament is Psalm 8, which takes the form of reflection on the place of humanity in the natural world. The psalmist considers the immensity of the night sky, before turning to consider the place of human beings in this vast universe:

> When I look at your heavens, the work of your fingers,
>   the moon and the stars that you have established;
> what are human beings that you are mindful of them,
>   mortals that you care for them?
>
> Yet you have made them a little lower than God,
>   and crowned them with glory and honor. (Ps. 8:3–5)

The passage locates humanity at a level that is intermediate between God and the beasts of the field.

This insight is supplemented by one of the most significant elements of the Christian narrative—namely, that God chooses to relate to human beings. God chose to enter into human history as one of us, in order to restore our broken relationship with God. The core Christian ideas of incarnation and atonement affirm that we matter to God, that we are sufficiently important to God to motivate this great drama of solidarity, restoration, and redemption. (We considered this point earlier in relation to C. S. Lewis's sermon about God diving into the world to save humanity; see "Explaining Significance: Narrating the Incarnation" in chap. 3.) To be created in the image of God is a privilege, yet it is a still greater privilege to be redeemed by God. As John Donne put this in one of his Holy Sonnets:

> 'Twas much, that man was made like God before,
> But, that God should be made like man, much more.[40]

Once more, the apologist is called on to explore how best to express and communicate such ideas to a wider audience. What analogies might be used to illuminate these issues? What stories might be told to help communicate the points at issue?

Purpose: Why Am I Here?

Many people regard the search for personal and communal authenticity and fulfillment as being of central and critical importance. The idea that Christianity both articulates and enables such fulfillment was present from its outset. Christianity presented itself not as an enemy of Judaism (within which it initially emerged) but as representing its climax and fulfillment. Christ's declaration in the Sermon on the Mount was widely seen as a manifesto of this position: "Do not think that I have come to abolish the Law or the Prophets; I have not come to abolish them but to fulfill them" (Matt. 5:17 NIV).

Yet Christianity rapidly established itself in Roman and Greek culture in the late first century, so that its relationship with Judaism gradually came to be seen as of diminishing relevance. Many early Christian writers presented Christianity as the fulfillment of the classic human quest for wisdom and highlighted the way in which Christianity resonated with themes in the writings of philosophers such as Plato and Plotinus. Other early Christian writers located the significance of Christianity at a more existential level.

For Augustine of Hippo, Christianity offered a vision of a God who was able to fulfill the deepest longings of the human heart. This is expressed in his famous prayer: "You have made us for yourself, and our heart is restless until it finds its rest in you."[41] The fundamental theme here is that human beings have some built-in longing to relate to God (an idea often articulated in terms of bearing the "image of God"), so that finding and embracing God is thus about becoming what we are meant to be and experiencing joy and peace in doing so. It is through embracing and entering the Christian narrative that we find purpose.

As might be expected, this theme is found throughout C. S. Lewis's Chronicles of Narnia. The Chronicles of Narnia resonate deeply with the basic human intuition that our own story is part of something grander—which, once grasped, allows us to see our situation in a new and more meaningful way. A veil is lifted, or a door is opened, so that we enter a new realm. Our own story is now seen to be part of a much bigger story, which helps us both to understand how we fit into a greater scheme of things and to discover and value the difference we can make. Lewis deftly shows how individual narratives acquire both value and purpose through becoming part of a greater narrative. Each character advances the story of Narnia in his or her own distinct way, thus becoming part of an ongoing and unfolding story that discloses and affirms each character's own distinct purpose.

One of the more disturbing implications of atheist interpretations of the theory of evolution is that we are here by accident, the outcome of a cosmic happenstance. This conclusion is not, it must be stressed, demanded by evolutionary biology itself; it is the outcome of the fusion of the basic themes of evolutionary biology with an aggressive and dogmatic atheism. Yet it is an unsettling thought, even for many atheists who profess to believe it. Some, of course, argue that its metaphysical austerity is an indicator of its truth. When I was an atheist myself, I took a certain pride in believing in such grim and bleak ideas, seeing it as a badge of intellectual courage and integrity. I would have echoed Steven Weinberg's view that the natural sciences disclose a meaningless universe: "The more the universe seems comprehensible, the more it seems pointless."[42]

Bleakness, however, can hardly be considered to be a reliable indicator of truth. The Christian narrative makes a counterassertion: God is the heart's true desire, the goal of our longings, and the fulfiller of our deepest aspirations. The philosopher Pascal thus saw human longing as a pointer to our true goal:

What else does this longing and helplessness proclaim, but that there was once in each person a true happiness, of which all that now remains is the empty print and trace? We try to fill this in vain with everything around us, seeking in things that are not there the help we cannot find in those that are there. Yet none can change things, because this infinite abyss can only be filled with something that is infinite and unchanging—in other words, by God himself. God alone is our true good.[43]

The Christian narrative provides a rich and deeply satisfying answer to the profound questions that we ask ourselves about the meaning of life. The Christian tradition has developed many ways of expressing this belief. The "chief end" of human existence, according to the Westminster Shorter Catechism (1648), is "to enjoy God," while giving God glory. The Christian narrative thus gives us a sense of purpose, allowing us to see how we fit into a greater picture of reality and can play a meaningful role in advancing it. It allows us to see ourselves as created by God in such a way that we find joy and fulfillment in relating to God.

The apologist thus has a rich range of narrative resources, above all stories of how individuals have found purpose in life and the difference that this has made to them. Some of the material here may be helpful in taking these matters further; each apologist, however, is best advised to develop her own range of resources as she develops her ministry.

Agency: Can I Make a Difference?

Finally, we need to consider an important yet often neglected question: Can I make a difference? Or am I so insignificant and powerless that I might as well not be here? Or are we, as Richard Dawkins declares, "robot vehicles blindly programmed to preserve the selfish molecules known as genes"?[44] The capacity to choose to make a difference is seen by many people as integral to their quest for meaning and purpose. If I cannot choose to make a difference, I might as well not be here. The issue is that of empowerment. Do we have what it takes to make a difference? Or is this something we need to be enabled to do, drawing on something that lies beyond us in doing so?

Michael Horton uses a helpful analogy in reflecting on the Christian "meganarrative," suggesting that believers "are no longer spectators but are actually included in the cast" of this drama.[45] The point to appreciate here is that through faith Christian believers become part of God's unfolding story. We must think of ourselves as graciously invited to become part of this cast and thus being made capable of undertaking roles of real importance in developing God's story, no matter how insignificant these might appear from a purely human perspective.[46] It is within this narrative that our real identity emerges and develops.

To have faith is thus to accept the invitation to step inside this story-shaped world, which both transforms our understanding of our place in the physical world of our habitation and brings about a "new creation" (2 Cor. 5:17) as we are transformed by grace. We now see ourselves as wayfarers passing through this world, assured of our citizenship and right of abode in the renewed and transformed reality that we call "heaven." While knowing that we are frail, wounded, and broken, we also know that we are under the care of a healing and restoring God. We know that we do not travel on our own, but in the company of a journeying God who shepherds us through life, remaining with us and being there for us even when we pass through the "valley of the shadow of death" (Ps. 23:4 KJV).

The Christian narrative helps us grasp that human nature is damaged and wounded by sin and not able to achieve its full potential unaided. It is a point made throughout the New Testament, particularly in the writings of Paul: "I can will what is right, but I cannot do it. For I do not do the good I want, but the evil I do not want is what I do" (Rom. 7:18–19). Paul was convinced that he was trapped, unable to break free from the prison of his own limitations and weaknesses. What could be done? In the end, Paul found his answer: "Who will rescue me from this body of death? Thanks be to God through Jesus Christ our Lord!" (Rom. 7:24–25).

This theme was subsequently developed by Augustine of Hippo, who was fully alert to the problem of human weakness, fragility, and brokenness.[47] For Augustine, human beings are damaged by sin, which is like a hereditary disease, passed down from one generation to another, that weakens humanity and cannot be cured by human agency. Christ is the divine physician, by whose "wounds we are healed" (Isa. 53:5 NIV). We are thus healed by the grace of God, so that our minds may recognize God and our wills may respond to the divine offer of grace.

Or, to change the image, sin is like a power that holds us captive and from whose grip we are unable to break free by ourselves. The human free will is captivated by the power of sin and may be liberated only by grace. Christ is thus seen as the liberator, the source of the grace that breaks the power of sin. Or again, sin is a type of guilt or moral impurity that is passed down from one generation to another. Christ thus comes to bring forgiveness and pardon. Using such images, Augustine builds a powerful depiction of human nature being weakened, impoverished, and trapped by sin—but healed and liberated by grace. A Christian account of human agency thus recognizes the importance of seeking to attain virtue, while setting the question of human agency within the dialectic of sin and grace.

Yet some will rightly raise a question here. Does not the notion of divine grace subvert both the idea of human agency and the moral basis of the pursuit of virtue? In a careful and thoughtful reflection on this point, N. T. Wright argues for a virtue ethic that is "generated and sustained by grace," within which human agency is seen as enabled by grace. He thus excludes "any suggestion that the 'virtue' we are going to talk about is something that 'we do' through self-effort."[48] God's grace enables us to become the people we are meant to be, so that "our journey is not one of achievement but of implementation, not of unaided goodness but of unmerited grace."[49] Wright sums up this narrative approach as follows: "The Christian teaching and practice of virtue, then, can be understood in terms of the life that is lived within the story whose goal, whose *telos*, is that complete, redeemed, renewed and perfected human life. . . . Love is not our duty; it is our *destiny*."[50]

There is an interesting parallel here with Karl Marx asserting the historical inevitability of socialism while still affirming the important role of individual socialists in bringing this about.[51] Human agency was not abolished nor subverted by the inevitability of this goal; rather, the inevitability of this goal meant that human agents could commit to this political struggle in hope, knowing that their commitment was not in vain.

> Although it is inevitable that a socialist revolution will come, it is not inevitable how long it will take for it to come, nor how painful its course will be. It may therefore be rational for revolutionaries to dedicate themselves to the socialist movement, so that they will be in a position to shorten, and to reduce the severity, of the "birth pangs" of socialism.[52]

There are, of course, problems with Marx's approach, not least in that the "inevitability" of socialism now seems indefensible. It is certainly possible to argue that moral agents can act rationally and responsibly, even when their actions are undertaken on behalf of a goal whose achievement they believe to be inevitable. However, it is questionable that the inevitability of this goal being achieved makes it moral or even appropriate to work for such a goal.

Wright, however, does not see the inevitability of the Christian *telos* as a justification for human agency; rather, he locates this within an eschatological framework. It is the anticipation in the present of what is hoped for in the future. By setting human agency within a Pauline narrative framework of present grace and future hope, Wright avoids the difficulties Marx encountered. Paul's concept of the renewal of the mind (Rom. 12:2) thus opens the way to transformed moral behavior through transformed ways of thinking.[53] The Christian believer is not a passive beholder of another's actions but rather has become an active agent in God's world.

In this chapter, we have considered four core elements of the human understanding of "meaning" and reflected on how they connect with the Christian metanarrative, noting in particular how this narrative is intrinsically capable of generating and justifying such concepts of meaning. They are not imposed upon this narrative but emerge from within it. Each of the four elements of meaning considered in this section is likely to resonate with different individuals, to different extents. Yet this is the outcome of the richness of the Christian "grand story," which an apologist should be able to connect with the individual needs and concerns of different audiences, rather than offering a generalized approach lacking any particularization.

7.

Handing Over: Developing Narrative Approaches to Apologetics

This short book is a manifesto for narrative apologetics—for the joyful, creative, and faithful use of stories to communicate and commend the central truths of the Christian gospel. These truths are not abstract propositional ideas but the living reality of people whose lives have been enriched and redirected through the encounter with a living and loving God. They can speak of how they have truly been transformed by a graceful and gracious God, in and through Jesus Christ. The natural response to such a transformative encounter is to tell the story of what has happened and the difference that it has made. And at one level, that's what narrative apologetics is all about.

Some readers will find the approach adopted in this book to be strange, others to be challenging. But I suspect many (especially preachers) will find that it resonates with both their deepest intuitions and their personal experience. When asked to explain what the gospel is, we tell a story. When asked to explain what difference the gospel makes to life, we tell a story. That's not where the discussion will end, but it is where it most appropriately begins.

I often use an analogy in trying to open up the rich complexity of the Christian faith, whether this is framed in terms of its narrative elements or its core doctrinal components. Great British scientist Isaac Newton showed that a beam of sunlight, when passed through a glass prism, is broken down into a spectrum of its constituent colors—red, orange, yellow, green, blue, indigo, and violet. Yet the prism does not create those colors; it merely allows them to be separated out from each other, so that they can be seen individually. Similarly, the individual elements of Christianity's rich and complex metanarrative can be set out and explored individually, so that their apologetic significance and value can be assessed. The Christian "grand story" is made up of interwoven and integrated "little stories." This book has offered some explorations of these "little stories"—but others can easily be added or developed.

Many have argued that the value of an artistic work or a worldview is measured by its capacity to engage fully and simultaneously all our mental capacities—cognitive, emotional, imaginative, and perceptual.[1] A narrative approach to apologetics opens up these four core aspects of the Christian gospel, allowing us to engage the human imagination and feelings in a deeply satisfying way, which older rational approaches to apologetics are unable to do. By making good use of narratives, the apologist can help others grasp how the Christian faith informs and nourishes our minds, captivates our hearts and imaginations, and inspires and motivates our actions in the world.

Having set out this manifesto for narrative apologetics, I must now hand it over to my readers and invite them to take things further for themselves. I have passed on a set of tools; it is up to you to decide how you use them. Readers of my earlier work *Mere Apologetics* have expressed particular appreciation for the suggestions I make in that work about how they might develop their own distinctive approaches. In bringing this work to an end, I shall repeat this pattern.

Using Biblical Narratives

I have made extensive use of biblical narratives throughout this work, including the great stories of the exodus and the exile (see "The Story of the Exodus: The Hope of Deliverance" and "The Story of the Exile: Where Do We Really Belong?" in chap. 4), as well as what is perhaps the greatest story ever told—the life, death, and resurrection of Jesus Christ (see "The Story of Jesus Christ: Rendering the Love of God" in chap. 4). Yet there is much more that could be done with the narratives of the exodus and the exile. I have merely scratched the surface of their rich deposits of meaning and significance. Furthermore, there are many other biblical stories that are rich in apologetic potential and can easily find their place in apologetic sermons, addresses, and conversations. Narratives possess a remarkable ability to cross a generational divide and speak to both adults and children.[2]

Might I offer an exercise to my readers? I invite you to consider, on the basis of the ideas developed in this book, what apologetic points you could make by telling and retelling the following biblical stories:

1. Isaiah's vision of the glory of God (Isa. 6:1–8)
2. Jesus calming the storm on Lake Galilee (Mark 4:35–41)
3. Jesus's encounter with Zacchaeus (Luke 19:1–10)
4. Jesus's encounter with the Samaritan woman (John 4:1–42)
5. The parable of the woman and the lost coin (Luke 15:8–10)
6. The parable of the prodigal son (Luke 15:11–32)
7. Paul's visit to the Areopagus (Acts 17:16–34)

In each case the task is to tell the story in ways that capture your audience's attention and imagination and to work the angles of the narrative to connect with the hopes and longings of your listeners.

Or you can develop this approach and use a contemporary retelling of a biblical narrative as a way of opening up the core themes of the original narrative for a contemporary audience. You might like to explore these possibilities:

1. C. S. Lewis's *Magician's Nephew* (1955) as a window into the biblical creation narrative (Gen. 1)
2. William Golding's *Lord of the Flies* (1954) as a window into the biblical narrative of the fall (Gen. 3)[3]
3. Marilynne Robinson's *Gilead* (2004) as a window into the parable of the prodigal son (Luke 15:11–32)

This approach can be taken further. There is no shortage of works that can act as windows into the grand narrative of faith *as a whole* (rather than individual biblical passages). For example, Madeleine L'Engle's *Wrinkle in Time* (1962) and J. K. Rowling's *Harry Potter and the Deathly Hallows* (2007) both open up some major apologetic themes for discussion by raising questions that invite correlation with the Christian "big picture" as a whole. The list is not difficult to extend!

Using Personal Narratives

Each of us has a story to tell. One of the reasons I love reading biographies (and sometimes writing them as well) is because it helps me to understand how the core ideas of Christianity change people, by becoming part of their lives. People are not containers filled with ideas; they are living realities whose existence is changed by the ideas they embody.

Those stories need to be told, and their significance appreciated. There is good biblical precedent for telling our stories as a way of demonstrating the ability of the gospel to change lives, thus affirming that it is life changing, not simply evidence based or reasonable. For example, consider how Paul responded to criticism he faced in Jerusalem. He offered an *apologia* by telling his story (Acts 22:1–21).[4] That story is of a life-changing encounter with the risen Christ that both motivated his evangelistic ministry and undergirded his fundamental conviction of the truth of the Christian faith. Something happened to Paul that redirected the course of his life and the shape of his beliefs—and that "something" can be set out only in the form of a narrative.[5]

By telling our stories, we bear witness to the capacity of the gospel to give us direction in life to cope with uncertainty and difficulty and to live well and meaningfully in what so often seems a confusing world. As I have suggested in this book, the personal narratives of individual Christians have enormous apologetic potential. They depend not on verbal brilliance for their appeal but on the fact that they are real-life accounts of truthful and faithful living. A personal narrative might serve as a testimony to the capacity of the gospel to change some lives and give stability and purpose to others. A personal narrative has an inner authenticity and a rhetorical power that far exceed those of a logical argument, even though they can both be linked together in a creative and persuasive whole.

The challenge that a preacher or speaker thus faces is deciding which personal narratives are best adapted to bridge the intellectual and experiential gap between the gospel and the audience. Such a decision will ultimately be based on knowing the audience to be addressed, as well as the personal narratives that are available. And since it is not entirely satisfactory to tell someone else's story, those narratives are best told by their subjects. Seekers are looking for people whose message resonates authentically with their manner and way of life, in effect seeing someone's quality of life as a measure of the validity of the person's ideas.[6] This may not make much intellectual sense to those raised within a rationalist culture—but we have to learn how others evaluate worldviews and respond appropriately. Apologists may have been late in discovering the importance of what is now known as "emotional intelligence," but its importance for their task can hardly be overlooked.[7]

Using Cultural Narratives

The range of narratives at our disposal is vast. In addition to the rich repository of biblical stories and the personal narratives of individual believers, the apologist can draw on cultural narratives such as literature and films. The range of literary writers engaged in this short work is somewhat limited. It is not difficult to see why I have used C. S. Lewis so often. Lewis clearly gave considerable thought to narrative approaches to apologetics and offered both important and helpful reflections on the theological foundations of these approaches and examples of how they might be developed further. Yet there are other writers who might well offer alternative approaches, capable of enriching and expanding the limited account presented in this work. I have no doubt that the literary writings of Dorothy L. Sayers and Marilynne Robinson—touched on but not fully developed in this work—offer an embarrassment of riches to the narrative apologist, and I suspect that many others might also be explored with great profit.

Yet this is simply the tip of the iceberg. Some will feel that my literary examples are sociologically limited. I will freely confess that this is indeed the case! But this range of writing can easily and productively be extended by others, sensitive to the needs and opportunities of their cultural contexts, and aware of the cultural narratives that are known to and can connect with those contexts.

Readers will know their own audiences well and can easily draw selectively and appropriately on the narratives of novels and movies to open up the great questions of life and explore Christian responses.

This short book has offered an introduction—and nothing more than an introduction—to the emerging field of narrative apologetics, aiming to open up its potentially rich and fertile pastures for exploration and inhabitation. I hope that it will encourage others to explore and develop this rich resource for Christian ministry and outreach. It is a manifesto, using broad brush strokes to depict the theological foundations and apologetic possibilities of this approach.

Yet fine brushwork is clearly needed if this approach is to be developed further. It is obvious, for example, that more attention needs to be given to providing a theological explanation of the role that stories play in so many aspects of human existence. We also need a better empirical understanding of how stories work in creating receptivity to new ideas or alternative ways of understanding our world. There is also a pressing theological need for deeper reflection on how the Christian narrative functions as a medium or agent of salvation, not merely of revelation. Yet my hope is that enough has been said to allow readers to appreciate the possibilities that this approach opens up and to explore how it can be developed further. There is so much more to explore!

Notes

Chapter 1 Introducing Narrative Apologetics

1. Ursula K. Le Guin, *Language of the Night: Essays on Fantasy and Science Fiction* (New York: Berkley, 1982), 22.

2. For the accessibility and imaginative stimulus of the Gospel narratives for children, see Melody R. Briggs, *How Children Read Biblical Narrative: An Investigation of Children's Readings of the Gospel of Luke* (Eugene, OR: Pickwick, 2017).

3. Marilynne Robinson, *Gilead* (London: Virago, 2005), 203.

4. See, for example, Margaret R. Somers, "The Narrative Constitution of Identity: A Relational and Network Approach," *Theory and Society* 23 (1994): 605–49; Elinor Ochs and Lisa Capps, "Narrating the Self," *Annual Review of Anthropology* 25 (1996): 19–43; Crystal L. Park, "Religion as a Meaning-Making Framework in Coping with Life Stress," *Journal of Social Issues* 61, no. 4 (2005): 707–29; Joshua A. Hicks and Laura A. King, "Meaning in Life and Seeing the Big Picture: Positive Affect and Global Focus," *Cognition and Emotion* 21, no. 7 (2007): 1577–84; Jonathan Gottschall, *The Storytelling Animal: How Stories Make Us Human* (Boston: Houghton Mifflin Harcourt, 2012). My focus in this book is on the narrative quality of human experience and existence, rather than on narrative *as a literary genre*.

5. Edmund Arens, "'Wer kann die großen Taten des Herrn erzählen?' (Ps 106, 2): Die Erzählstruktur christlichen Glaubens in systematischer Perspektive," in *Erzählter Glaube—Erzählende Kirche*, ed. Rolf Zerfass, 13–27 (Freiburg: Herder, 1988); my translation.

6. John Stephens and Robyn McCallum, *Retelling Stories, Framing Culture: Traditional Story and Metanarratives in Children's Literature* (New York: Garland, 1998), 3–23.

7. Stephen Crites, "The Narrative Quality of Experience," *Journal of the American Academy of Religion* 39, no. 3 (1971): 291–311; Lewis P. Hinchman and Sandra K. Hinchman, eds., *Memory, Identity, Community: The Idea of Narrative in the Human Sciences* (Albany: State University of New York Press, 1997).

8. Jeffry R. Halverson, H. L. Goodall, and Steven R. Corman, "What Is a Master Narrative?," in *Master Narratives of Islamist Extremism*, 11–26 (New York: Palgrave Macmillan, 2011).

9. For this phrase, see Stanley E. Fish, *Is There a Text in This Class? The Authority of Interpretive Communities* (Cambridge, MA: Harvard University Press, 1980), 147–74.

10. Rowan Williams, *Resurrection: Interpreting the Easter Gospel*, 2nd ed. (London: Darton, Longman & Todd, 2002), 61–62.

11. Charles Taylor, *Modern Social Imaginaries* (Durham, NC: Duke University Press, 2002), 23.

12. Gilbert Meilaender, "Theology in Stories: C. S. Lewis and the Narrative Quality of Experience," *Word and World* 1, no. 3 (1981): 222–30.

13. Christopher J. H. Wright, *The Mission of God: Unlocking the Bible's Grand Narrative* (Downers Grove, IL: InterVarsity, 2006), 29–69.

14. Gwilym H. Jones, *The Nathan Narratives* (Sheffield: JSOT Press, 1990), 93–118.

15. For the influence of the Enlightenment on the emergence of evangelicalism, see David W. Bebbington, "Evangelical Christianity and Modernism," *Crux* 26, no. 2 (1990): 1–9.

16. This concern is noted in Donald G. Bloesch, "Evangelical Rationalism and Propositional Revelation," *Reformed Review* 51, no. 3 (1998): 169–81. Although Bloesch sees Carl F. H. Henry (1913–2003) as an important influence in sidelining the narrative aspects of the Bible, caution needs to be exercised at this point, as noted by Chad Owen Brand, "Is Carl Henry a Modernist? Rationalism and Foundationalism in Post-War Evangelical Theology," *Southern Baptist Journal of Theology* 8, no. 4 (2004): 44–60.

17. J. I. Packer, *"Fundamentalism" and the Word of God* (London: Inter-Varsity, 1958), 101–14.

18. For an excellent defense of this point, see Gunda Schneider-Flume, "Die vielen Geschichten der biblischen Tradition und die eine Geschichte Gottes: Zur Frage nach Einheit und Mitte der Schrift," in *Dogmatik erzählen? Die Bedeutung des Erzählens für eine biblisch orientierte Dogmatik*, ed. Gunda Schneider-Flume and Doris Hiller, 31–50 (Neukirchen-Vluyn: Neukirchener Verlag, 2005).

19. For possible ways of integrating such multiple narratives, see Tom Billington, "Constructing Critical Resources for Research and Professional Practice with Young People: Feeling, Thinking, Learning, and Neuroscientific Narratives," *Qualitative Research in Psychology* 10 (2013): 174–88.

20. Christian Smith, *Moral, Believing Animals: Human Personhood and Culture* (Oxford: Oxford University Press, 2009), 63–94.

21. Alister E. McGrath, *Enriching Our Vision of Reality: Theology and the Natural Sciences in Dialogue* (West Conshohocken, PA: Templeton Foundation Press, 2017). More specifically, see Alister E. McGrath, "Narratives of Significance: Reflections on the Engagement of Anthropology and Christian Theology," in *Theologically Engaged Anthropology: Social Anthropology and Theology in Conversation*, ed. J. Derrick Lemons, 123–39 (New York: Oxford University Press), 2018.

22. Stanley Hauerwas, "On Keeping Ethics Theological," in *Against the Nations: War and Survival in a Liberal Society*, 23–50 (Notre Dame, IN: University of Notre Dame Press, 1992).

23. Stanley Hauerwas, *In Good Company: The Church as Polis* (Notre Dame, IN: University of Notre Dame Press, 1995), 41.

24. Stanley Hauerwas, "The Demands of a Truthful Story: Ethics and the Pastoral Task," *Chicago Studies* 21, no. 1 (1982): 59–71.

25. Michael Goldberg, *Theology and Narrative: A Critical Introduction* (Nashville: Abingdon, 1982), 35 (my emphasis).

26. Goldberg, *Theology and Narrative*, 35 (emphasis in original).

27. Timothy P. Burt, "Homogenising the Rainfall Record at Durham for the 1870s," *Hydrological Sciences Journal* 54, no. 1 (2009): 199–209.

28. J. R. de Laeter et al., "Atomic Weights of the Elements: Review 2000 (IUPAC Technical Report)," *Pure and Applied Chemistry* 75, no. 6 (2003): 683–800.

29. Alister E. McGrath, *C. S. Lewis—A Life: Eccentric Genius, Reluctant Prophet* (Carol Stream, IL: Tyndale, 2013), 351–52.

30. For some helpful perspectives, see Craig van Gelder, "From the Modern to the Postmodern in the West: Viewing the Twentieth Century in Perspective," *Word & World* 20, no. 1 (2000): 32–40.

31. For the impact of this development on religious belief, see Christian Smith and Brandon Vaidyanathan, "Multiple Modernities and Religion," in *Oxford Handbook of Religious Diversity*, ed. Chad Meister, 250–65 (New York: Oxford University Press, 2010).

32. This does not mean that it is no longer important to affirm the truthfulness of the Christian faith; it is rather to recognize that this is no longer the primary question that preoccupies many in Western culture.

33. Alister E. McGrath, *Mere Apologetics: How to Help Seekers and Skeptics Find Faith* (Grand Rapids: Baker Books, 2011), 13–25.

34. John Gray, *Seven Types of Atheism* (London: Penguin, 2018), 9–10.

35. Bertrand Russell, *A History of Western Philosophy* (London: George Allen & Unwin, 1946), xiv.

36. Karl Barth, *Table Talk*, ed. J. D. Godsey (Edinburgh: Oliver & Boyd, 1963), 62.

37. On this theme, see Alister E. McGrath, *Mere Discipleship: Growing in Wisdom and Hope* (Grand Rapids: Baker Books, 2019).

38. These three Greek words are difficult to translate into English but roughly mean "reason."

39. Krista C. McCormack, "Ethos, Pathos, and Logos: The Benefits of Aristotelian Rhetoric in the Courtroom," *Washington University Jurisprudence Review* 7, no. 1 (2014): 131–55.

40. Note the very limited use made of narrative in Plato: Stephen Halliwell, "The Theory and Practice of Narrative in Plato," in *Narratology and Interpretation: The Content of Narrative Form in Ancient Literature*, ed. Jonas Grethlein and Antonios Rengakos, 15–41 (Berlin: De Gruyter, 2009).

41. Peter T. Struck, "The Invention of Mythic Truth in Antiquity," in *Antike Mythen: Medien, Transformationen und Konstruktionen*, ed. Ueli Dill and Christine Walde, 25–37 (Berlin: De Gruyter, 2009).

42. Robert L. Fowler, "Mythos and Logos," *Journal of Hellenic Studies* 131 (2011): 45–66.

43. Austin Farrer, "The Christian Apologist," in *Light on C. S. Lewis*, ed. Jocelyn Gibb, 23–43 (London: Geoffrey Bles, 1965), here 26.

44. Ian James Kidd, "Epistemic Vices in Public Debate: The Case of 'New Atheism,'" in *New Atheism: Critical Perspectives and Contemporary Debates*, ed. Christopher Cotter, Philip Quadrio, and Jonathan Tuckett, 51–68 (Dordrecht: Springer Verlag, 2017).

45. Christopher Hitchens, *God Is Not Great: How Religion Poisons Everything* (New York: Twelve, 2007), 5.

46. Drusilla Scott, *Everyman Revived: The Common Sense of Michael Polanyi* (Grand Rapids: Eerdmans, 1995), 60.

47. For discussion, see Alister E. McGrath, "An Enhanced Vision of Rationality: C. S. Lewis on the Reasonableness of Christian Faith," *Theology* 116, no. 6 (2013): 410–17.

48. C. S. Lewis, "Is Theology Poetry?," in *Essay Collection* (London: Collins, 2000), 21.

49. Mark Bevir, "Narrative as a Form of Explanation," *Disputatio* 9 (2000): 10–18. For the role of narrative explanations in the natural sciences, see Stephen P. Norris, Sandra M. Guilbert, Martha L. Smith, Shahram Hakimelahi, and Linda M. Phillips, "A Theoretical Framework for Narrative Explanation in Science," *Science Education* 89, no. 4 (2005): 535–63.

50. J. David Velleman, "Narrative Explanation," *Philosophical Review* 112, no. 1 (2003): 1–25, here 1. More generally, see Ismay Barwell, "Understanding Narratives and Narrative Understanding," *Journal of Aesthetics and Art Criticism* 67, no. 1 (2009): 49–59.

51. Noël Carroll, "On the Narrative Connection," in *New Perspectives on Narrative Perspective*, ed. Willie van Peer and Seymour B. Chatman, 21–41 (Albany: State University of New York Press, 2001).

52. Wesley C. Salmon, *Causality and Explanation* (Oxford: Oxford University Press, 1998), 320–29.

53. See Anya Plutynski, "Explanatory Unification and the Early Synthesis," *British Journal for Philosophy of Science* 56 (2005): 595–609; Rebecca Schweder, "A Defense of a Unificationist Theory of Explanation," *Foundations of Science* 10 (2005): 421–35.

54. See the early study of Stephen J. Read, "Constructing Accounts: The Role of Explanatory Coherence," in *Explaining Oneself to Others: Reason Giving in a Social Context*, ed. M. L. McLaughlin, M. J. Cody, and S. J. Read, 3–19 (Hillsdale, NJ: Erlbaum, 1992).

55. Marilynne Robinson, *What Are We Doing Here?* (New York: Farrar, Straus & Giroux, 2018), 257.

56. C. S. Lewis, *Surprised by Joy* (London: HarperCollins, 2002), 197.

57. Michael F. Steger, "Meaning in Life," in *Oxford Handbook of Positive Psychology*, ed. Shane J. Lopez, 679–87 (Oxford: Oxford University Press, 2009).

58. Robert A. Emmons, *The Psychology of Ultimate Concerns: Motivation and Spirituality in Personality* (New York: Guilford Press, 1999).

59. See, for example, Joshua Seachris, "The Meaning of Life as Narrative: A New Proposal for Interpreting Philosophy's 'Primary' Question," *Philo* 12, no. 1 (2009): 5–23.

60. W. V. O. Quine, *From a Logical Point of View*, 2nd ed. (Cambridge, MA: Harvard University Press, 1951), 20–46.

61. G. K. Chesterton, "The Return of the Angels," *Daily News*, March 14, 1903.

62. Chesterton, "Return of the Angels."

63. See Alister E. McGrath, "The Privileging of Vision: Lewis's Metaphors of Light, Sun, and Sight," in *The Intellectual World of C. S. Lewis*, 83–104 (Oxford: Wiley-Blackwell, 2013).

64. C. S. Lewis to Arthur Greeves, October 18, 1931, in *The Collected Letters of C. S. Lewis*, 3 vols., ed. Walter Hooper (San Francisco: HarperOne, 2004–6), 1:977.

65. Michael Bamberg, "Who Am I? Narration and Its Contribution to Self and Identity," *Theory & Psychology* 21, no. 1 (2011): 3–24.

66. Lewis P. Hinchman and Sandra K. Hinchman, eds., *Memory, Identity, Community: The Idea of Narrative in the Human Sciences* (Albany: State University of New York Press, 1997).

67. Jonathan Gottschall, *The Storytelling Animal: How Stories Make Us Human* (Boston: Houghton Mifflin Harcourt, 2012), 87–116.

68. Joseph Henderson, "Ancient Myth and Modern Man," in Carl G. Jung, *Man and His Symbols*, 104–57 (New York: Doubleday, 1964).

69. Joseph Campbell and Bill D. Moyers, *The Power of Myth* (New York: Doubleday, 1988).

70. Stuart Voytilla, *Myth and the Movies: Discovering the Mythic Structure of 50 Unforgettable Films* (Studio City, CA: Michael Wiese Productions, 1999).

71. J. R. R. Tolkien, *Tree and Leaf* (London: HarperCollins, 2001), 56.

72. Tolkien, *Tree and Leaf*, 71–72.

73. Alister E. McGrath, "The Enigma of Autobiography: Critical Reflections on *Surprised by Joy*," in *The Intellectual World of C. S. Lewis*, 7–30 (Oxford: Wiley-Blackwell, 2013).

74. McGrath, *C. S. Lewis—A Life*, 146–51.

75. C. S. Lewis to Arthur Greeves, October 18, 1931, in *Collected Letters*, 1:977.

76. Lewis to Arthur Greeves, October 18, 1931, in *Collected Letters*, 1:977.

77. Bruce Lincoln, *Theorizing Myth: Narrative, Ideology, and Scholarship* (Chicago: University of Chicago Press, 1999), 47–140.

78. Eric Csapo, *Theories of Mythology* (Oxford: Blackwell, 2005), 292–93.

79. Lewis, "Myth Became Fact," in *Essay Collection*, 142.

Chapter 2 The Theological Foundations of Narrative Apologetics

1. N. T. Wright, *The New Testament and the People of God* (Minneapolis: Fortress, 1992), 41–42.
2. See, for example, George W. Stroup, *The Promise of Narrative Theology: Recovering the Gospel in the Church* (Atlanta: John Knox Press, 1981).
3. H. Richard Niebuhr, *The Meaning of Revelation* (New York: Macmillan, 1960), 43–90.
4. Niebuhr, *Meaning of Revelation*, 43.
5. Niebuhr, *Meaning of Revelation*, 47–48.
6. Niebuhr, *Meaning of Revelation*, 45.
7. Niebuhr, *Meaning of Revelation*, 59–60.
8. Niebuhr, *Meaning of Revelation*, 90.
9. Niebuhr, *Meaning of Revelation*, 93.
10. Niebuhr, *Meaning of Revelation*, 109.
11. Niebuhr, *Meaning of Revelation*, 110–12.
12. Niebuhr, *Meaning of Revelation*, 120.
13. Niebuhr, *Meaning of Revelation*, 125.
14. Niebuhr, *Meaning of Revelation*, 126.
15. Niebuhr, *Meaning of Revelation*, 38–39.
16. Niebuhr, *Meaning of Revelation*, 93.
17. See Gordon E. Michaelson Jr., "Theology, Historical Knowledge, and the Contingency-Necessity Distinction," *International Journal for Philosophy of Religion* 14 (1983): 87–98, with especial reference to the view of the leading Enlightenment writer G. E. Lessing that the "contingent truths of history can never become the proof of the necessary truths of reason."
18. Two seminal German articles should be noted, both in the same edition of the journal *Concilium*: Harald Weinrich, "Narrative Theologie," *Concilium* 9 (1973): 329–34; and Jean-Baptiste Metz, "Kleine Apologie des Erzählens," *Concilium* 9 (1973): 334–42. German-speaking theology has developed this idea in its own distinct manner: see, for example, Gunda Schneider-Flume and Doris Hiller, eds., *Dogmatik erzählen? Die Bedeutung des Erzählens für eine biblisch orientierte Dogmatik* (Neukirchen-Vluyn: Neukirchener Verlag, 2005). My discussion in this work draws primarily on English-language scholarship.
19. Hans Frei, *The Eclipse of Biblical Narrative: A Study in Eighteenth and Nineteenth Century Biblical Hermeneutics* (New Haven: Yale University Press, 1977), 51–65. Note especially Frei's comments on prevalent perceptions about the relation of myth and narrative (267–81).
20. Frei, *Eclipse of Biblical Narrative*, 15–16.
21. See the important analysis in Richard B. Hays, *The Faith of Jesus Christ: The Narrative Substructure of Galatians 3:1–4:11*, 2nd ed. (Grand Rapids: Eerdmans, 2002).
22. Stanley Hauerwas, *A Community of Character: Towards a Constructive Christian Social Ethic* (Notre Dame, IN: University of Notre Dame Press, 1991), 67.
23. These are set out clearly in David K. Clark, "Narrative Theology and Apologetics," *Journal of the Evangelical Theological Society* 36 (1993): 499–515.

24. This issue was discussed extensively at the 1995 Wheaton College Theology Conference: "Evangelicals and Postliberals in Conversation." For my contribution to this conference, see Alister E. McGrath, "An Evangelical Evaluation of Postliberalism," in *The Nature of Confession: Evangelicals & Postliberals in Conversation*, ed. Timothy R. Phillips and Dennis L. Okholm, 23–44 (Downers Grove, IL: InterVarsity, 1996).

25. Donald G. Bloesch, "Evangelical Rationalism and Propositional Revelation," *Reformed Review* 51, no. 3 (1998): 173.

26. A good starting point is N. T. Wright, *Scripture and the Authority of God: How to Read the Bible Today* (San Francisco: HarperOne, 2013). For a different approach, see Kevin J. Vanhoozer, *The Drama of Doctrine: A Canonical-Linguistic Approach to Christian Theology* (Louisville: Westminster John Knox, 2005).

27. C. S. Lewis, *Selected Literary Essays* (Cambridge: Cambridge University Press, 1969), 265.

28. Gary Comstock, "Truth or Meaning: Ricoeur versus Frei on Biblical Narrative," *Journal of Religion* 66, no. 2 (1986): 117–41. See also Gary Comstock, "Two Types of Narrative Theology," *Journal of the American Academy of Religion* 55, no. 4 (1987): 687–717.

29. Edward T. Oakes, "Apologetics and the Pathos of Narrative Theology," *Journal of Religion* 72, no. 1 (1992): 37–58.

30. As noted by Comstock, "Truth or Meaning."

31. See the points made by David K. Clark, "Narrative Theology and Apologetics," *Journal of the Evangelical Theological Society* 36 (1993): 499–515. For some evangelical concerns about narrative theology, see Carl F. H. Henry, "Narrative Theology: An Evangelical Appraisal," *Trinity Journal* 8, no 1 (1987): 3–19.

32. Alasdair C. MacIntyre, *Whose Justice? Which Rationality?* (London: Duckworth, 1988), 350.

33. L. Gregory Jones, "Rhetoric, Narrative, and the Rhetoric of Narratives: Exploring the Turns to Narrative in Recent Thought and Discourses," *Issues in Integrative Studies* 11 (1993): 7–25.

34. For some recent examples of this approach, see Adam Sparks, "The Fulfilment Theology of Jean Daniélou, Karl Rahner and Jacques Dupuis," *New Blackfriars* 89 (2008): 633–56.

35. Jean-François Lyotard, *The Postmodern Condition: A Report on Knowledge* (Manchester: Manchester University Press, 1992), xxvi–xxv.

36. See Merold Westphal, *Overcoming Onto-Theology: Toward a Postmodern Christian Faith* (New York: Fordham University Press, 2001), xi–xvii. For a more expansive response to this issue, see the excellent study of James K. A. Smith, *Who's Afraid of Postmodernism? Taking Derrida, Lyotard, and Foucault to Church* (Grand Rapids: Baker Academic, 2006), esp. 59–79.

37. Frances Young, "Augustine's Hermeneutics and Postmodern Criticism," *Interpretation* 58, no. 1 (2004): 42–55.

38. J. Smith, *Who's Afraid of Postmodernism?*, 23.

39. See Alister E. McGrath, *The Territories of Human Reason: Science and Theology in an Age of Multiple Rationalities* (Oxford: Oxford University Press,

2019). This work echoes some of the themes found in Karl-Otto Apel and Matthias Kettner, eds., *Die eine Vernunft und die vielen Rationalitäten* (Frankfurt am Main: Suhrkamp, 1996).

40. An ideology can be understood as an "attempt to represent the universal from the particular point of view of the dominant class" in such a way that this artificial social construction seems eminently reasonable and natural; see Claude Lefort, *The Political Forms of Modern Society: Bureaucracy, Democracy, Totalitarianism* (Cambridge, MA: MIT Press, 1986), 200.

41. Michael S. Horton, *The Christian Faith: A Systematic Theology for Pilgrims on the Way* (Grand Rapids: Zondervan, 2011), 17.

42. J. R. R. Tolkien, *Tree and Leaf* (London: HarperCollins, 2001), 56. See further Verlyn Flieger, *Splintered Light: Logos and Language in Tolkien's World* (Kent, OH: Kent State University, 2002).

43. Richard L. Purtill, *J. R. R. Tolkien: Myth, Morality, and Religion* (San Francisco: Ignatius Press, 2003), 16–44.

44. C. S. Lewis, "Myth Became Fact," in *Essay Collection* (London: Collins, 2000), 142.

45. Lewis, "Is Theology Poetry?," in *Essay Collection*, 16.

46. Lewis, "Is Theology Poetry?," in *Essay Collection*, 16.

47. Lewis, "Is Theology Poetry?," in *Essay Collection*, 16.

48. Ragner Holte, "*Logos Spermatikos*: Christianity and Ancient Philosophy according to St. Justin's Apologies," *Studia Theologica* 12, no. 1 (1958): 109–68. More recently, see Mark J. Edwards, *Image, Word, and God in the Early Christian Centuries* (Farnham, UK: Ashgate, 2013).

49. Fabienne Claire Caland, "Le *mythos spermatikos*," in *Horizons du mythe*, ed. Denise Brassard and Fabienne Claire Caland, 7–32 (Montréal: Cahiers du CELAT, 2007).

50. Dorothy L. Sayers, *The Mind of the Maker* (London: Methuen, 1941), 15–24. For comment, see Alister E. McGrath, *Mere Discipleship: Growing in Wisdom and Hope* (Grand Rapids: Baker Books, 2019), 73–84.

51. Sayers, *Mind of the Maker*, 172–73.

52. Lewis, "The Seeing Eye," in *Essay Collection*, 59.

53. For a good example, see Cecilia Bosticco and Teresa L. Thompson, "Narratives and Story-Telling in Coping with Grief and Bereavement," *Omega* 51, no. 1 (2005): 1–16.

54. For two of the best, see Timothy Keller, *Walking with God through Pain and Suffering* (New York: Dutton, 2013); Eleonore Stump, *Wandering in Darkness: Narrative and the Problem of Suffering* (Oxford: Clarendon Press, 2010). Stump's criticism of technocratic philosophical approaches to suffering, which lack any sense of feeling with the subject, led her to explore narrative approaches as a way of reconnecting with real life, rather than getting lost in the technical abstractions and probabilistic algorithms that have become increasingly prominent in recent philosophical considerations of the problem of suffering.

55. For a good overview, see Peter J. Kreeft, *Making Sense out of Suffering* (Ann Arbor, MI: Servant, 1986).

56. G. R. Evans, *Augustine on Evil* (Cambridge: Cambridge University Press, 1990).

57. Ellen M. Ross, *The Grief of God: Images of the Suffering Jesus in Late Medieval England* (New York: Oxford University Press, 1997).

58. C. S. Lewis, *The Problem of Pain* (London: HarperCollins, 2002), 91.

59. Ann Loades, "C. S. Lewis: Grief Observed, Rationality Abandoned, Faith Regained," *Literature and Theology* 3 (1989): 107–21.

60. C. S. Lewis, *A Grief Observed* (New York: HarperCollins, 1994), 44.

61. Lewis, *Grief Observed*, 44.

62. Keller, *Walking with God*, 58.

Chapter 3 The Practical Application of Narrative Apologetics

1. Melody R. Briggs, *How Children Read Biblical Narrative: An Investigation of Children's Readings of the Gospel of Luke* (Eugene, OR: Pickwick, 2017), 33–52.

2. C. S. Lewis, "Sometimes Fairy Stories May Say Best What's to Be Said," in *Essay Collection* (London: Collins, 2000), 527–28.

3. Gilbert Meilaender, "Theology in Stories: C. S. Lewis and the Narrative Quality of Experience," *Word and World* 1, no. 3 (1981): 228.

4. Rowan D. Williams, *The Lion's World: A Journey into the Heart of Narnia* (New York: Oxford University Press, 2013), 27.

5. Paul K. Moser, *The Evidence for God: Religious Knowledge Reexamined* (Cambridge: Cambridge University Press, 2010), 33–37.

6. C. S. Lewis, "Is Theology Poetry?," "Myth Became Fact," and "On Stories," in *Essay Collection*, 10–21, 138–42, 491–504.

7. This is not an entirely reliable interpretation of Feuerbach. It rests on George Eliot's translation of Feuerbach's *Essence of Christianity* (1841), which renders his German term *Vergegenstandigung* as "projection," where a more helpful translation would be "objectification." See Max W. Wartofsky, *Feuerbach* (Cambridge: Cambridge University Press, 1982), 206–10.

8. Sigmund Freud, *The Future of an Illusion* (New York: W. W. Norton, 1961), 30.

9. Thomas Nagel, *The Last Word* (Oxford: Oxford University Press, 1997), 130.

10. Sigmund Freud, *Complete Psychological Works*, 24 vols. (London: Vintage, 2001), 11:123.

11. See his "Biographical Critique of Freud's Atheism," in Paul C. Vitz, *Sigmund Freud's Christian Unconscious* (Grand Rapids: Eerdmans, 1993), 207–22.

12. C. S. Lewis to Nancy Warner, October 26, 1963, in *The Collected Letters of C. S. Lewis*, 3 vols., ed. Walter Hooper (San Francisco: HarperOne, 2004–6), 3:1472.

13. C. S. Lewis, *The Silver Chair* (London: HarperCollins, 2002), 143.

14. See D. Francois Tolmie, "Salvation as Redemption: The Use of 'Redemption' Metaphors in Pauline Literature," in *Salvation in the New Testament: Perspectives on Soteriology*, ed. Jan G. van der Watt, 247–69 (Leiden: Brill, 2005). See also Brenda B. Colijn, *Images of Salvation in the New Testament* (Downers Grove, IL: IVP Academic, 2010), 124–74.

15. Tolmie, "Salvation as Redemption," 262–66.

16. I discuss this and related analogies in Alister E. McGrath, *Mere Apologetics: How to Help Seekers and Skeptics Find Faith* (Grand Rapids: Baker Books, 2011), 128–30.

17. For this theme in Calvin, see J. Todd Billings, *Calvin, Participation, and the Gift: The Activity of Believers in Union with Christ* (Oxford: Oxford University Press, 2007), 42–64.

18. Roger Scruton, *The Face of God: The Gifford Lectures 2010* (London: Continuum, 2014), 45.

19. For an excellent account of this development, see Frances M. Young and Andrew Teal, *From Nicaea to Chalcedon: A Guide to the Literature and Its Background*, 2nd ed. (Grand Rapids: Baker Academic, 2010).

20. This was the famous view of Wilhelm Nestle, *Vom Mythos zum Logos: Die Selbstentfaltung des griechischen Denkens von Homer bis auf die Sophistik und Sokrates*, 2nd ed. (Stuttgart: Kröner, 1942). For an overdue corrective to the simplifications of Nestle's approach, see Robert L. Fowler, "Mythos and Logos," *Journal of Hellenic Studies* 131 (2011): 45–66.

21. Alister E. McGrath, *Christian Theology: An Introduction*, 6th ed. (Hoboken, NJ: Wiley-Blackwell, 2017), 207–24.

22. Dorothy L. Sayers, *Creed or Chaos?* (London: Methuen, 1947), 32–35.

23. C. S. Lewis, *The Lion, the Witch and the Wardrobe* (London: HarperCollins, 2002), 65.

24. See Williams, *Lion's World*, 49–73.

25. Lewis, "The Grand Miracle," in *Essay Collection*, 3–9.

26. Lewis, "The Grand Miracle," in *Essay Collection*, 4.

27. H. Richard Niebuhr, *The Meaning of Revelation* (New York: Macmillan, 1960), 123–24.

28. Marilynne Robinson, *What Are We Doing Here?* (New York: Farrar, Straus & Giroux, 2018), 271.

29. R. G. Collingwood, *An Autobiography* (London: Oxford University Press, 1939), 79.

30. John Gray, *Straw Dogs: Thoughts on Humans and Other Animals* (London: Granta, 2002), 29.

31. Gray, *Straw Dogs*, 14.

32. Rowan Williams, interview by Jeremy Paxman, *Newsnight*, BBC Two, September 15, 2009, quoted in Andrew Goddard, *Rowan Williams: His Legacy* (Oxford: Lion, 2013), 254.

33. Stanley Hauerwas and David Burrell, "From System to Story: An Alternative Pattern for Rationality in Ethics," in *The Roots of Ethics: Science, Religion, and Values*, ed. Daniel Callahan and H. Tristram Engelhardt Jr., 75–116 (New York: Plenum, 1981).

34. For the narrational aspects of this passage, see David J. Southall, *Rediscovering Righteousness in Romans: Personified Dikaiosynē within Metaphoric and Narratorial Settings* (Tübingen: Mohr Siebeck, 2008), 113–47.

35. Mark Roseman, *The Villa, the Lake, the Meeting: Wannsee and the Final Solution* (London: Penguin, 2003).

36. George Steiner, *Language and Silence: Essays 1958–1966* (London: Faber, 1967), 15.

37. For the story, see *The Saga of the Volsungs: The Norse Epic of Sigurd the Dragon Slayer*, trans. Jesse L. Byock (London: Penguin, 1999), 63–65.

38. C. S. Lewis, *The Voyage of the "Dawn Treader"* (London: HarperCollins, 2002), 105.

39. Lewis, *Voyage of the "Dawn Treader,"* 123.

Chapter 4 Biblical Narratives

1. For a good introduction, see N. T. Wright, *Scripture and the Authority of God: How to Read the Bible Today* (San Francisco: HarperOne, 2013).

2. The issues are ably summarized in Joel Edmund Anderson, "A Narrative Reading of Solomon's Execution of Joab in 1 Kings 1–2: Letting Story Interpret Story," *Journal for the Evangelical Study of the Old Testament* 1, no. 1 (2012): 43–62. The "Succession narrative" is generally held to consist of the extended block of text from 2 Samuel 9 to 1 Kings 2.

3. See especially the important analysis of the role of narrative in Paul's understanding of the gospel: N. T. Wright, *Paul and the Faithfulness of God* (London: SPCK, 2013), 475–85. For a critical assessment of this approach, see Joel R. White, "N. T. Wright's Narrative Approach," in *God and the Faithfulness of Paul: A Critical Examination of the Pauline Theology of N. T. Wright*, ed. Christoph Heilig, J. Thomas Hewitt, and Michael F. Bird, 181–206 (Tübingen: Mohr Siebeck, 2016).

4. Ludwig Wittgenstein, *Philosophical Investigations*, 4th ed. (Oxford: Wiley-Blackwell, 2009), §115.

5. David Egan, "Pictures in Wittgenstein's Later Philosophy," *Philosophical Investigations* 34, no. 1 (2011): 55–76.

6. Charles Taylor, *A Secular Age* (Cambridge, MA: Belknap Press, 2007), 25.

7. See the important essay in Gordon P. Baker, *Wittgenstein's Method: Neglected Aspects; Essays on Wittgenstein* (Malden, MA: Blackwell, 2004), 260–78.

8. Jan Assmann, *Moses the Egyptian* (Cambridge, MA: Harvard University Press, 2008), 34–35.

9. See the rich collection of material gathered in Thomas E. Levy, Thomas Schneider, and William H. C. Propp, eds., *Israel's Exodus in Transdisciplinary Perspective: Text, Archaeology, Culture and Geoscience* (Cham, Switzerland: Springer, 2015). A case can be made for the exodus dating to the thirteenth century BC during the Ramesside Period.

10. Cf. Josh. 24:17: "It is the LORD our God who brought us and our ancestors up from the land of Egypt, out of the house of slavery, and who did those great signs in our sight. He protected us along all the way that we went, and among all the peoples through whom we passed." For further discussion, see Brad E. Kelle, *Telling the Old Testament Story: God's Mission and God's People* (Nashville: Abingdon, 2017).

11. Nathalie LaCoste, "Writing the Exodus in Egypt: The Role of Place in Shaping Jewish Narratives," *Journal for the Study of the Pseudepigrapha* 25, no. 4 (2016): 274–98.

12. Frances M. Young, *Biblical Exegesis and the Formation of Christian Culture* (Cambridge: Cambridge University Press, 1997), 140–60.

13. Michael Cameron, "Augustine and Scripture," in *A Companion to Augustine*, ed. Mark Vessey, 200–214 (Oxford: Blackwell, 2012).

14. John Chrysostom, *Catacheses* 3.24.

15. For the original text of this sermon, see https://kinginstitute.stanford.edu /king-papers/documents/draft-chapter-viii-death-evil-upon-seashore.

16. Mary Midgley, *The Myths We Live By* (London: Routledge, 2004), 26–28.

17. See Louis Pojman, *Who Are We? Theories of Human Nature* (New York: Oxford University Press, 2005); Jonathan Jong and Aku Visala, "Three Quests for Human Nature: Some Philosophical Reflections," *Philosophy, Theology and the Sciences* 1, no. 2 (2014): 146–71.

18. See, for example, Scott M. Langston, *Exodus through the Centuries* (Malden, MA: Blackwell, 2006), 126–58; Tremper Longman, *How to Read Exodus* (Downers Grove, IL: IVP Academic, 2009), 143–74.

19. See Avraham Faust, "Deportation and Demography in Sixth-Century BCE Judah," in *Interpreting Exile: Displacement and Deportation in Biblical and Modern Contexts*, ed. Brad E. Kelle, Frank Ritchel Ames, and Jacob L. Wright, 91–104 (Atlanta: Society of Biblical Literature, 2011); Jonathan Stökl and Caroline Waerzeggers, eds., *Exile and Return: The Babylonian Context* (Berlin: De Gruyter, 2015).

20. See especially Rainer Albertz, *Israel in Exile: The History and Literature of the Sixth Century B.C.E.* (Leiden: Brill, 2004).

21. David M. Carr, "Jerusalem's Destruction and Babylonian Exile," in *Holy Resilience: The Bible's Traumatic Origins*, ed. David M. Carr, 67–90 (New Haven: Yale University Press, 2014).

22. Kurt Rudolph, *Gnosis: The Nature and History of Gnosticism* (San Francisco: Harper & Row, 1983), 33–34.

23. Blaise Pascal, *Pensées* (Mineola, NY: Dover, 2003), 61 (no. 205).

24. G. K. Chesterton, *Tremendous Trifles* (London: Methuen, 1909), 209.

25. "Riders on the Storm," on The Doors, *LA Woman*, Elektra K 42090, LP, 1971.

26. The historical records, of course, suggest that many of the exiles chose to stay in Babylon after Cyrus permitted them to return home.

27. For the history of Babylon as a literary trope, see Andrew P. Scheil, *Babylon under Western Eyes: A Study of Allusion and Myth* (Toronto: University of Toronto Press, 2016), 195–294.

28. Rikki Watts and David Pao see an "Isaianic new exodus" as a central motif of the Gospel of Mark and Acts, respectively; these seem to me to be overinterpretations of the biblical material. See Rikki E. Watts, *Isaiah's New Exodus and Mark* (Tübingen: Mohr Siebeck, 1997); David W. Pao, *Acts and the Isaianic New Exodus* (Grand Rapids: Baker Academic, 2000). There seems, however, good reason to suggest that Jesus is depicted as the messianic herald of Isaiah 52:7 or 61:1 at points: see R. T. France, *The Gospel of Mark: A Commentary on the Greek Text* (Grand Rapids: Eerdmans, 2002), 90–91.

29. For detailed comment, see G. Walter Hansen, *The Letter to the Philippians*, Pillar New Testament Commentary (Grand Rapids: Eerdmans, 2009), 267–77.

30. Hansen, *Letter to the Philippians*, 1–6.

31. *Epistle to Diognetus*, 5. This letter probably dates from the second century.

32. For the text and theological comment, see Alister E. McGrath, *Theology: The Basic Readings* (Hoboken, NJ: Wiley-Blackwell, 2018), 210–12.

33. Alister E. McGrath, "Reason, Experience, and Imagination: Lewis's Apologetic Method," in *The Intellectual World of C. S. Lewis*, 129–46 (Oxford: Wiley-Blackwell, 2013).

34. C. S. Lewis, *Mere Christianity* (London: HarperCollins, 2002), 136–37.

35. Alister E. McGrath, "Arrows of Joy: Lewis's Argument from Desire," in *The Intellectual World of C. S. Lewis*, 105–28 (Oxford: Wiley-Blackwell, 2013).

36. C. S. Lewis, *The Last Battle* (London: HarperCollins, 2004), 171.

37. Emil Brunner, *Wahrheit als Begegnung: Sechs Vorlesungen über das christliche Wahrheitsverständnis* (Zürich: Zwingli-Verlag, 1938), 34. For comment, see Alister E. McGrath, *Emil Brunner: A Reappraisal* (Oxford: Wiley-Blackwell, 2014), 166–69.

38. Brunner, *Wahrheit als Begegnung*, 105.

39. See especially Brian J. Wright, *Communal Reading in the Time of Jesus: A Window into Early Christian Reading Practices* (Minneapolis: Fortress, 2017).

40. For good discussions of this question, see Larry W. Hurtado, *Why on Earth Did Anyone Become a Christian in the First Three Centuries?* (Milwaukee: Marquette University Press, 2016), 46–108; Bart D. Ehrman, *The Triumph of Christianity* (New York: Simon & Schuster, 2017), 105–30.

41. John R. W. Stott, *The Cross of Christ* (Downers Grove, IL: InterVarsity, 1986), 174.

42. See, for example, the points made in Mitzi Kirkland-Ives, *In the Footsteps of Christ: Hans Memling's Passion Narratives and the Devotional Imagination in the Early Modern Netherlands* (Turnhout, Belgium: Brepols, 2013).

43. Klyne Snodgrass, *Stories with Intent: A Comprehensive Guide to the Parables of Jesus* (Grand Rapids: Eerdmans, 2018), 2.

44. Leander E. Keck, *A Future for the Historical Jesus: The Place of Jesus in Preaching and Theology* (Philadelphia: Fortress, 1981), 245–47.

45. David Stern, *Parables in Midrash: Narrative and Exegesis in Rabbinic Literature* (Cambridge, MA: Harvard University Press, 1994), 103–14.

46. Snodgrass, *Stories with Intent*, 205, 227.

47. For discussion, see Robert F. Capon, *Kingdom, Grace, Judgment: Paradox, Outrage, and Vindication in the Parables of Jesus* (Grand Rapids: Eerdmans, 2002), 113–23; Snodgrass, *Stories with Intent*, 248–60.

48. C. S. Lewis, "Myth Became Fact," in *Essay Collection* (London: Collins, 2000), 140.

49. See, for example, John Haldane, "Philosophy, the Restless Heart, and the Meaning of Theism," *Ratio* 19, no. 4 (2006): 421–40. For the importance of this theme in preaching, see the classic work of John Piper, *Desiring God: Meditations of a Christian Hedonist* (Colorado Springs: Multnomah, 2011).

50. See the helpful discussion of the "intuitions of the heart" in James R. Peters, *The Logic of the Heart: Augustine, Pascal, and the Rationality of Faith* (Grand Rapids: Baker Academic, 2009), 10, 16.

51. C. S. Lewis, *The Four Loves* (London: HarperCollins, 2002), 26–27.
52. Jeffrey Bilbro, "Phantastical Regress: The Return of Desire and Deed in *Phantastes* and *The Pilgrim's Regress*," *Mythlore* 28 (2010): 21–37.
53. C. S. Lewis, *The Pilgrim's Regress* (London: Geoffrey Bles, 1950), 10.
54. Lewis, *Pilgrim's Regress*, 10.
55. Marilynne Robinson, *Gilead* (New York: Farrar, Straus & Giroux, 2004); idem, *Home* (New York: Farrar, Straus & Giroux, 2008). For an excellent discussion, see Alison Jack, "Barth's Reading of the Parable of the Prodigal Son in Marilynne Robinson's *Gilead*: Exploring Christlikeness and Homecoming in the Novel," *Literature and Theology* 32, no. 1 (2018): 100–116.

Chapter 5 Strategies and Criteria for Narrative Apologetics

1. This second approach is explored in Brian Godawa, *Word Pictures: Knowing God through Story & Imagination* (Downers Grove, IL: InterVarsity, 2009).
2. See Rick Busselle and Helena Bilandzic, "Fictionality and Perceived Realism in Experiencing Stories: A Model of Narrative Comprehension and Engagement," *Communication Theory* 18, no. 2 (2008): 255–80.
3. C. S. Lewis, "The Weight of Glory," in *Essay Collection* (London: Collins, 2000), 99.
4. The view of Karl Barth. For the development of this argument, see Stanley Hauerwas, *With the Grain of the Universe: The Church's Witness and Natural Theology* (Grand Rapids: Brazos, 2001).
5. See Charles Taylor, "The Church Speaks—to Whom?," in *Church and People: Disjunctions in a Secular Age*, ed. Charles Taylor, Jose Casanova, and George F. McLean, 17–24 (Washington, DC: Council for Research in Values and Philosophy, 2012). For Taylor's relevance to apologetics and the ministry of the churches, see James K. A. Smith, *How (Not) to Be Secular: Reading Charles Taylor* (Grand Rapids: Eerdmans, 2014).
6. Sam Keyes, "*How (Not) to Be Secular* – A Review," Bethinking, accessed September 25, 2018, https://www.bethinking.org/culture/how-not-to-be-secular-review.
7. J. Smith, *How (Not) to Be Secular*, 62.
8. Robert Wuthnow, *After Heaven: Spirituality in America since the 1950s* (Berkeley: University of California Press, 1998), 3–9.
9. Tomáš Halík, *Patience with God: The Story of Zacchaeus Continuing in Us* (New York: Doubleday, 2009), 77. The English translation of this title unfortunately fails to pick up the nuances of the original Czech, *Vzdáleným na blízku* (To stand by the distant).
10. Halík, *Patience with God*, 9. See further Tomáš Halík, "Church for the Seekers," in *A Czech Perspective on Faith in a Secular Age*, ed. Tomáš Halík and Pavel Hošek, 127–33 (Washington, DC: Council for Research in Values and Philosophy, 2015).
11. Oliver O'Donovan, *The Ways of Judgment: The Bampton Lectures, 2003* (Grand Rapids: Eerdmans, 2005), xiii.
12. O'Donovan, *Ways of Judgment*, xiii.

13. C. S. Lewis, *Surprised by Joy* (London: HarperCollins, 2002), 249.

14. Lewis, *Surprised by Joy*, 249.

15. Lewis, *Surprised by Joy*, 249.

16. J. R. R. Tolkien, *Tree and Leaf* (London: HarperCollins, 2001), 71–72.

17. Alasdair MacIntyre, *Three Rival Versions of Moral Enquiry: Encyclopedia, Genealogy, and Tradition* (Notre Dame, IN: University of Notre Dame Press, 1990), 81. MacIntyre attributes this approach to Dante.

18. For "progress as incorporation" in the development of scientific theories, see John Losee, *Theories of Scientific Progress: An Introduction* (New York: Routledge, 2004), 5–61. For unificationism as a form of scientific explanation, see Sorin Bangu, "Scientific Explanation and Understanding: Unificationism Reconsidered," *European Journal for Philosophy of Science* 7, no. 1 (2017): 103–26.

19. This topic is covered in standard textbooks, such as C. L. Tang, *Fundamentals of Quantum Mechanics* (Cambridge: Cambridge University Press, 2005). For some accessible reflections on the theological relevance of such developments, see John C. Polkinghorne, *Quantum Physics and Theology: An Unexpected Kinship* (London: SPCK, 2007), 48–72.

20. For comment, see Abraham Pais, *Niels Bohr's Times, in Physics, Philosophy and Polity* (Oxford: Clarendon Press, 1991), 192–96.

21. See, for example, N. P. Landsman, *Mathematical Topics between Classical and Quantum Mechanics* (New York: Springer, 1998), 7–10; Franz Gross, *Relativistic Quantum Mechanics and Field Theory* (New York: Wiley, 1999), 18–22.

22. Alister E. McGrath, "The Rationality of Faith: How Does Christianity Make Sense of Things?," *Philosophia Christi* 18, no. 2 (2016): 395–408.

23. Alister E. McGrath, "A Gleam of Divine Truth: The Concept of Myth in Lewis's Thought," in *The Intellectual World of C. S. Lewis*, 55–82 (Oxford: Wiley-Blackwell, 2013).

24. For analysis and comment, see Alvin Plantinga, *Where the Conflict Really Lies: Science, Religion, and Naturalism* (New York: Oxford University Press, 2011); Alister E. McGrath, *The Big Question: Why We Can't Stop Talking about Science, Faith, and God* (New York: St. Martins Press, 2015); the UK edition of *The Big Question* was published as *Inventing the Universe: Why We Can't Stop Talking about Science, Faith and God* (London: Hodder & Stoughton, 2015).

25. Dawkins's ridiculous vilification in *The God Delusion* of the atheist philosopher Michael Ruse as such an "appeaser" has been the subject of widespread derision: Richard Dawkins, *The God Delusion* (London: Bantam, 2006), 66–69.

26. J. A. Froude, *Short Studies on Great Subjects* (London: Longmans, Green, 1898), 1.

27. Christopher Hitchens, *God Is Not Great: How Religion Poisons Everything* (New York: Twelve, 2007), 47.

28. Cary P. Gross and Kent A. Sepkowitz, "The Myth of the Medical Breakthrough: Smallpox, Vaccination, and Jenner Reconsidered," *International Journal of Infectious Diseases* 3 (1998): 54–60.

29. George M. Marsden, *A Short Life of Jonathan Edwards* (Grand Rapids: Eerdmans, 2008), 131.

30. For reflections on Shaw's disturbing misjudgment, see Sally Peters, "Commentary: Bernard Shaw's Dilemma; Marked by Mortality," *International Journal of Epidemiology* 32, no. 6 (2003): 918–19.

31. See especially Ronald L. Numbers, ed., *Galileo Goes to Jail and Other Myths about Science and Religion* (Cambridge, MA: Harvard University Press, 2009).

32. John Gray, *Seven Types of Atheism* (London: Penguin, 2018), 9.

33. For the historical complexities of narratives concerning science and religion, see Peter Harrison, *The Territories of Science and Religion* (Chicago: University of Chicago Press, 2015). One of the works that precipitated the cultural dominance of the "warfare" image was Andrew Dickson White, *A History of the Warfare of Science with Theology in Christendom*, 2 vols. (London: Macmillan, 1896).

34. For such an approach, see McGrath, *The Big Question*.

35. See especially Gilbert Meilaender, "Theology in Stories: C. S. Lewis and the Narrative Quality of Experience," *Word and World* 1, no. 3 (1981). Also relevant to this discussion are Louis Markos, *Restoring Beauty: The Good, the True, and the Beautiful in the Writings of C. S. Lewis* (Colorado Springs: Biblica, 2010); Michael Ward, "The Good Serves the Better and Both the Best: C. S. Lewis on Imagination and Reason in Apologetics," in *Imaginative Apologetics: Theology, Philosophy, and the Catholic Tradition*, ed. Andrew Davison, 59–78 (London: SCM Press, 2011).

36. Christian Smith, *Moral, Believing Animals: Human Personhood and Culture* (Oxford: Oxford University Press, 2009), 63–94.

37. See especially Peter Lipton, *Inference to the Best Explanation*, 2nd ed. (London: Routledge, 2004).

38. Paul R. Thagard, "The Best Explanation: Criteria for Theory Choice," *Journal of Philosophy* 75 (1978): 76–92; David H. Glass, "Coherence Measures and Inference to the Best Explanation," *Synthese* 157 (2007): 275–96.

39. C. Smith, *Moral, Believing Animals*, 64.

40. C. Smith, *Moral, Believing Animals*, 87.

41. Stanley Hauerwas, *A Community of Character: Towards a Constructive Christian Social Ethic* (Notre Dame, IN: University of Notre Dame Press, 1991), 9–35.

42. This same basic theme is explored in both N. T. Wright, *The Day the Revolution Began: Reconsidering the Meaning of Jesus's Crucifixion* (San Francisco: HarperOne, 2016), and Michael S. Horton, *The Christian Faith: A Systematic Theology for Pilgrims on the Way* (Grand Rapids: Zondervan, 2011), 35–220.

43. See, for example, Horton, *Christian Faith*.

44. Wright, *Day the Revolution Began*, 74–76. These ideas are developed further in N. T. Wright, *Surprised by Hope: Rethinking Heaven, the Resurrection, and the Mission of the Church* (New York: HarperOne, 2014).

45. Jonathan Aitken, *Charles W. Colson: A Life Redeemed* (Colorado Springs: Waterbrook, 2005), 192–211. For the wider impact of Lewis's classic work, see George M. Marsden, *C. S. Lewis's "Mere Christianity": A Biography* (Princeton: Princeton University Press, 2016).

46. We have already noted C. S. Lewis's attempt to facilitate the visualization of sin in *The Voyage of the "Dawn Treader"* (see "Translation and Transposition: Visualizing Sin" in chap. 3).

47. See, for example, Cecilia Bosticco and Teresa L. Thompson, "Narratives and Story-Telling in Coping with Grief and Bereavement," *Omega* 51, no. 1 (2005): 1–16.

48. Iris Murdoch, *Metaphysics as a Guide to Morals* (London: Penguin, 1992), 7.

49. See especially Peter J. Conradi, *The Saint and the Artist: A Study of the Fiction of Iris Murdoch* (London: HarperCollins, 2001).

50. Franco Moretti, "The Slaughterhouse of Literature," *Modern Language Quarterly* 61, no. 1 (2000): 207–27.

51. This is widely recognized as a core characteristic of detective fiction, which "exhibits narrative purity and intelligibility, having fully coherent stories with clear beginnings and closure at endings, in contrast to other modern fiction." See Alan H. Goldman, "The Appeal of the Mystery," *Journal of Aesthetics and Art Criticism* 69, no. 3 (2011): 261–72, here 263.

52. See especially Dorothy L. Sayers, *Les origines du roman policier* (Hurstpierpoint, UK: Dorothy L. Sayers Society, 2003).

53. Michael Goldberg, *Theology and Narrative: A Critical Introduction* (Nashville: Abingdon, 1982), 242.

54. Sayers, *Les origines du roman policier*, 14.

55. Barbara Reynolds, ed., *The Letters of Dorothy L. Sayers: Child and Woman of Her Time* (Hurstpierpoint, UK: Dorothy L. Sayers Society, 2002), 97.

56. Catherine M. Kenney, *The Remarkable Case of Dorothy L. Sayers* (Kent, OH: Kent State University Press, 1990), 53–119.

Chapter 6 The Christian Story and the Meaning of Life

1. Jeanette Winterson, *Why Be Happy When You Could Be Normal?* (London: Vintage, 2012), 68.

2. Crystal L. Park and Ian A. Gutierrez, "Global and Situational Meanings in the Context of Trauma: Relations with Psychological Well-Being," *Counselling Psychology Quarterly* 26, no. 1 (2013): 8–25.

3. Rainer Funk, *Erich Fromm: His Life and Ideas* (New York: Continuum, 2003).

4. Viktor E. Frankl, *Man's Search for Meaning: An Introduction to Logotherapy*, 4th ed. (Boston: Beacon Press, 1992). See further Paul T. P. Wong, "Viktor Frankl's Meaning-Seeking Model and Positive Psychology," in *Meaning in Positive and Existential Psychology*, ed. Alexander Batthyany and Pninit Russo-Netzer, 149–84 (New York: Springer, 2014).

5. Joanna Collicutt McGrath, "Post-Traumatic Growth and the Origins of Early Christianity," *Mental Health, Religion and Culture* 9 (2006): 291–306.

6. See Karl Popper, "Natural Selection and the Emergence of Mind," *Dialectica* 32 (1978): 342.

7. José Ortega y Gasset, "El origen deportivo del estado," *Citius, Altius, Fortius* 9, no. 1–4 (1967): 259–76.

8. Peter B. Medawar and Jean Medawar, *The Life Science: Current Ideas of Biology* (London: Wildwood House, 1977), 171.

9. Peter B. Medawar, *The Limits of Science* (Oxford: Oxford University Press, 1986), 76.

10. Nicholas Rescher, *The Limits of Science* (Berkeley: University of California Press, 1984), 209–10.

11. Salman Rushdie, *Is Nothing Sacred? The Herbert Read Memorial Lecture* (Cambridge: Granta, 1990), 8–9.

12. Keith Yandell, *Philosophy of Religion: A Contemporary Introduction* (London: Routledge, 1999), 16.

13. On the importance of this point for the scientific study of religion, see Jonathan Jong, "On (Not) Defining (Non)Religion," *Science, Religion and Culture* 2, no. 3 (2015): 15–24.

14. For example, see William E. Paden, "Theaters of Worldmaking Behaviors: Panhuman Contexts for Comparative Religion," in *Comparing Religions: Possibilities and Perils?*, ed. Thomas Idinopulos, Brian C. Wilson, and James C. Hanges, 59–76 (Leiden: Brill, 2006).

15. From an evangelical perspective, see Arthur Holmes, *Contours of a Christian Worldview* (Grand Rapids: Eerdmans, 1983); Peter S. Heslam, *Creating a Christian Worldview: Abraham Kuyper's Lectures on Calvinism* (Grand Rapids: Eerdmans, 1998); James W. Sire, *Naming the Elephant: Worldview as a Concept* (Downers Grove, IL: InterVarsity, 2004).

16. André F. Droogers, "The World of Worldviews," in *Methods for the Study of Religious Change*, ed. André F. Droogers and Anton van Harskamp, 17–42 (London: Equinox, 2014).

17. Mark E. Koltko-Rivera, "The Psychology of Worldviews," *Review of General Psychology* 8, no. 1 (2004): 3–58, here 4.

18. On this "universal Darwinism," see Richard Dawkins, "Darwin Triumphant: Darwinism as Universal Truth," in *A Devil's Chaplain: Selected Essays*, 78–90 (London: Weidenfield & Nicolson, 2003).

19. Mary Midgley, *Evolution as a Religion: Strange Hopes and Stranger Fears*, 2nd ed. (London: Routledge, 2002), 17–18.

20. Kristin L. Sommer, Roy F. Baumeister, and Tyler F. Stillman, "The Construction of Meaning from Life Events: Empirical Studies of Personal Narratives," in *The Human Quest for Meaning: Theories, Research, and Applications*, ed. Paul T. P. Wong, 297–314 (New York: Routledge, 2012).

21. For further discussion of the incarnational aspects of the "embodiment of meaning," see Alister E. McGrath, "Christianity: The Embodiment of Meaning," in *Philosophies of Life*, ed. Massimo Pigliucci, Skye Cleary, and Daniel A. Kaufman (New York: Vintage, 2019).

22. Donatella Pallotti, "'Out of Their Owne Mouths'? Conversion Narratives and English Radical Religious Practice in the Seventeenth Century," *Journal of Early Modern Studies* 1, no. 1 (2012): 73–95.

23. Pallotti, "'Out of Their Owne Mouths'?," 74.

24. Robert A. Emmons, *The Psychology of Ultimate Concerns: Motivation and Spirituality in Personality* (New York: Guilford Press, 1999). On the specific role of narratives in this process, see Dan P. McAdams, "Narrative Identity," in *Handbook*

of Identity Theory and Research, ed. Seth J. Schwartz, Koen Luyckx, and Vivian L. Vignoles, 99–115 (New York: Springer, 2011).

25. Roy Baumeister, *Meanings of Life* (New York: Guilford Press, 1991), 29–57. See further Michael J. MacKenzie and Roy F. Baumeister, "Meaning in Life: Nature, Needs, and Myth," in *Meaning in Positive and Existential Psychology*, ed. Alexander Batthyany and Pninit Russo-Netzer, 25–38 (New York: Springer, 2014).

26. Martin Buber, *I and Thou* (New York: Touchstone, 1996), 68.

27. Maurice S. Friedman, *Martin Buber: The Life of Dialogue*, 4th ed. (London: Routledge, 2002).

28. See, e.g., Stanley Hauerwas, *A Community of Character: Towards a Constructive Christian Social Ethic* (Notre Dame, IN: University of Notre Dame Press, 1991).

29. See especially Peter H. W. Lau, *Identity and Ethics in the Book of Ruth: A Social Identity Approach* (Berlin: De Gruyter, 2011).

30. Athena E. Gorospe, *Narrative and Identity: An Ethical Reading of Exodus 4* (Leiden: Brill, 2007).

31. Raymond Carver, "Late Fragment," in *All of Us: The Collected Poems* (London: Harvill Press, 1996), 294.

32. Sigmund Freud, "One of the Difficulties of Psycho-Analysis," *Journal of Mental Science* 67 (1921): 34–39.

33. Francis Crick, *The Astonishing Hypothesis: The Scientific Search for the Soul* (London: Simon & Schuster, 1994), 3, 11.

34. For a detailed discussion of Dawkins's views, see Alister E. McGrath, *Dawkins' God: From "The Selfish Gene" to "The God Delusion,"* 2nd ed. (Oxford: Wiley-Blackwell, 2014).

35. Richard Dawkins, *River out of Eden: A Darwinian View of Life* (London: Weidenfeld & Nicholson, 2015), 133.

36. Richard Dawkins, *The Selfish Gene*, 2nd ed. (Oxford: Oxford University Press, 1989), 21.

37. Dawkins, *Selfish Gene*, 200–201.

38. George Herbert, *Works*, ed. F. E. Hutchinson (Oxford: Clarendon, 1941), 184. For theological comment, see Alister E. McGrath, "The Alchemy of Grace: The Gospel and the Transformation of Reality in George Herbert's *Elixir*," in *The Passionate Intellect: Christian Faith and the Discipleship of the Mind* (Downers Grove, IL: InterVarsity, 2010), 45–55.

39. See, e.g., Julian of Norwich, *Revelations of Divine Love*, trans. Barry Windeatt, Oxford World's Classics (Oxford: Oxford University Press, 2015).

40. John Donne, *Selected Poems* (London: Penguin, 2006), 184.

41. Augustine of Hippo, *Confessions*, trans. Henry Chadwick (Oxford: Oxford University Press, 2008), 3.

42. Steven Weinberg, *The First Three Minutes: A Modern View of the Origin of the Universe* (New York: Basic Books, 1977), 154. A similar view is set out in Alex Rosenberg, *An Atheist's Guide to Reality: Enjoying Life without Illusions* (New York: Norton, 2011).

43. Blaise Pascal, *Pensées* (Mineola, NY: Dover, 2003), 425.

44. Dawkins, *Selfish Gene*, vii.

45. Michael S. Horton, *The Christian Faith: A Systematic Theology for Pilgrims on the Way* (Grand Rapids: Zondervan, 2011), 19.

46. Much the same point is made in Paul's analogy of the "body of Christ"; all members are important to its proper functioning and well-being, no matter how lowly they may seem (1 Cor. 12:12–27).

47. See Alister McGrath, *Heresy: A History of Defending the Truth* (San Francisco: HarperOne, 2009), 159–70.

48. N. T. Wright, "Faith, Virtue, Justification, and the Journey to Freedom," in *The Word Leaps the Gap: Essays on Scripture and Theology in Honor of Richard B. Hays*, ed. J. Ross Wagner, C. Kavin Rowe, and A. Katherine Grieb (Grand Rapids: Eerdmans, 2008), 473.

49. Wright, "Faith, Virtue, Justification," 478.

50. Wright, "Faith, Virtue, Justification," 480.

51. See the valuable study of G. A. Cohen, "Historical Inevitability and Human Agency in Marxism," *Proceedings of the Royal Society of London A* 407, no. 1832 (1986): 65–87.

52. Cohen, "Historical Inevitability," 66.

53. Wright, "Faith, Virtue, Justification," 491.

Chapter 7 Handing Over

1. For example, Alan H. Goldman, *Aesthetic Value* (Boulder, CO: Westview, 1995).

2. See the way of enabling children to grasp the significance of biblical narratives set out in Jerome Berryman, *Godly Play: A Way of Religious Education* (San Francisco: HarperSanFrancisco, 1991), 42–59.

3. There is some useful material in Marijke van Vuuren, "Good Grief: Lord of the Flies as a Post-War Rewriting of Salvation History," *Literator* 25, no. 2 (2004): 1–25.

4. The Greek word *apologia* (Acts 22:1) is usually translated as "defense." For the way in which Paul conducted such defenses in a theologically informed manner, yet within the parameters of accepted Roman legal conventions, see Bruce W. Winter, "Official Proceedings and the Forensic Speeches in Acts 24–26," in *The Book of Acts: Ancient Literary Setting*, ed. Bruce W. Winter and Andrew D. Clarke, 305–36 (Grand Rapids: Eerdmans, 1994).

5. For the various versions of this narrative and their significance, see N. T. Wright, *Paul: A Biography* (San Francisco: HarperOne, 2018), 41–59.

6. Glen G. Scorgie, "Confrontational Apologetics versus Grace-Filled Persuasion," *Perichoresis* 10, no. 1 (2012): 23–39.

7. See, for example, Daniel M. Johnson and Adam C. Pelser, "Affective Apologetics: Communicating Truth through Humor, Ridicule, and Emotions," *Christian Research Journal* 35, no. 6 (2012): 44–48; Adam C. Pelser, "Reasons of the Heart: Emotions in Apologetics," *Christian Research Journal* 38, no. 1 (2015): 34–39.

Alister E. McGrath is the Andreas Idreos Professor of Science and Religion at Oxford University and director of the Ian Ramsey Centre for Science and Religion. He holds Oxford doctorates in the natural sciences, intellectual history, and Christian theology. McGrath has written extensively on the interaction of science and Christian theology and is the author of many books, including *Mere Discipleship*, *Mere Apologetics*, and the award-winning *C. S. Lewis—A Life*. McGrath also served as the Gresham Professor of Divinity, a public professorship in the City of London, established in 1597, that promotes the public engagement of theology with the leading issues of the day.

Cultivating a Christian Vision for All of Life

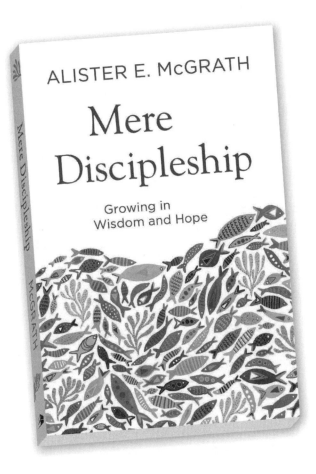

"Alister McGrath invariably combines enormous scholarship with an accessible and engaging style."

—Rowan Williams, master of Magdalene College,
University of Cambridge

Engage Skeptics with Intelligence and Imagination

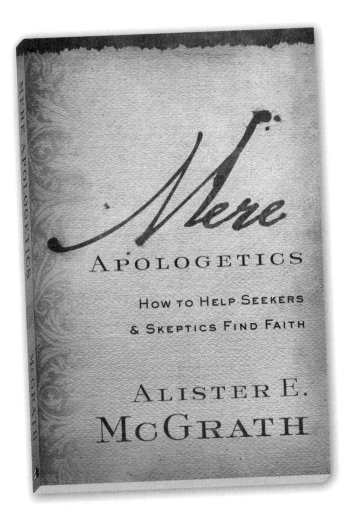

"This is a fresh, clear, and practical introduction to apologetics from someone who doesn't just talk about the subject but actually does it brilliantly."

—Os Guinness, author of *Long Journey Home*

A COMPREHENSIVE TOOL TO ENRICH YOUR BIBLE STUDY, TOPIC BY TOPIC

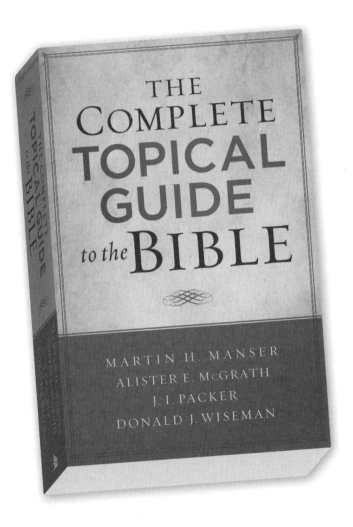

Connect with

BakerBooks

Relevant. Intelligent. Engaging.

Sign up for announcements about new and upcoming titles at

BakerBooks.com/SignUp

@ReadBakerBooks